MAKING SENSE OF SMOOT-HAWLEY

MAKING SENSE OF SMOOT-HAWLEY

TECHNOLOGY AND TARIFFS

Bernard C. Beaudreau

iUniverse, Inc.
New York Lincoln Shanghai

MAKING SENSE OF SMOOT-HAWLEY
TECHNOLOGY AND TARIFFS

iUniverse books may be ordered through booksellers or by contacting:

iUniverse
2021 Pine Lake Road, Suite 100
Lincoln, NE 68512
www.iuniverse.com
1-800-Authors (1-800-288-4677)

ISBN-13: 978-0-595-37888-3 (pbk)
ISBN-13: 978-0-595-82259-1 (ebk)
ISBN-10: 0-595-37888-9 (pbk)
ISBN-10: 0-595-82259-2 (ebk)

Printed in the United States of America

To the memory of Reed Smoot, for whom fear was never a factor.

On his return to Utah in August 1932, in preparation for his final battle in political life, Smoot advised his people that it had been the common attitude in 1930 to attribute the depression to unwise governmental policies, with the Smoot-Hawley act specified. Lest there were some obsessed with heresy, he declared, "To hold the American tariff policy, or any other policy of our government, responsible for this gigantic deflationary move is only to display one's ignorance of its sweeping universal character." He found that "The world is paying for its ruthless destruction of life and property in the World War and for its failure to adjust purchasing power to productive capacity during the industrial revolution of the decade following the war."

—Milton Merill, *Reed Smoot: Apostle in Politics*

Contents

Preface

The human response to adversity can be seen as a heuristic or a series of heuristics that is, reactions, responses, and policies that are untried, but that, intuitively, hold out much promise. Some are successful, others not. Some are remembered as strokes of genius, others not. Some go on to mold our collective identity, others not. Some are forgotten, relegated to the dark side of a nation's collective memory. This book is about one such heuristic, namely the Smoot-Hawley Tariff Act of 1930. Seen by many as folly, as log-rolling gone awry, as a symbol of the pitfalls of the U.S. political process, as a mistake, this book sheds new light on this critical period in U.S. economic history. Far from being misguided, shortsighted, and xenophobic, the Smoot-Hawley Tariff Bill of 1929 is shown to be a legitimate, but ill-fated response to the conditions of excess capacity brought about by the electrification of America, and the failure on the part of income to rise commensurately with output, a condition known as underincome.

I would like to thank those who over the years provided comments and criticisms on earlier drafts and related papers. All remaining errors are my sole responsibility.

Introduction

In recent times, however, the process by which new technological developments are transmitted into higher standards of living is obviously not working smoothly. Even before the coming of the great depression, there appeared to be some doubt as to whether the system of wealth production and distribution was operating with maximum effectiveness. At a time when cumulative scientific knowledge might be expected to give us an accelerating tempo of industrial growth, the rate of advancement for some reason, or combination of reasons did not seem to be an increasing one. In any case, the issue in recent years has been sharply raised: can the economic system be counted upon to produce the beneficent economic results which were supposed to be the automatic accompaniment of scientific knowledge, and the increasing efficiency of production? Under modern conditions, do not technological improvements simply throw men out of work, destroy purchasing power, and retard economic advancement?

—Spurgeon Bell, *Productivity, Wages and National Income*

Drafted by Senator Reed Smoot of Utah and Representative Willis C. Hawley of Oregon, the Smoot-Hawley Tariff Bill of 1929 called for unprecedented increases in U.S. tariffs on imports of food and manufactures, increasing the already high rates put in place seven years earlier under the auspices of the Fordney-McCumber Tariff Act of 1922.

Attempts to understand, let alone rationalize, this "defining moment" in the history of what, at the time, was the wealthiest nation on the face of the earth, have raised more questions than they have answered. For example, Frank Taussig and E. E. Shattschneider have argued that the Smoot-Hawley Tariff was the product of pressure group politics, specifically, of pressure group politics going amok. Others such as Pastor (1980) and Destler (1986) argue that tariff legislation in the 1920s was due to "party politics," specifically to the GOP's historic penchant for protectionism.

Left unanswered, however, are a number of critical issues. Until now, the debate over the Smoot-Hawley Tariff Act has focused, for the most part, on form, as opposed to substance. Rather than examining the demand for protection and the contributing factors in the 1920s, the debate has focused on the process, specifically on the process of tariff revision in the United States Congress. Did something change in the 1920s, something that, relative to conditions in the 1910s, increased the demand for protection on the part of manufacturers and farmers? Or was the latter infinite, with the elections of 1928 providing yet another opportunity for the Republican Party to ratchet up rates even higher? This only serves to raise other questions. For example, if the demand for protection was infinite, then why did Reed Smoot, the architect of the Fordney-McCumber Tariff Act, choose not to ratchet tariffs up to 1929 levels in 1922? Why not simply close the U.S. market to foreign imports of manufactures and food?

There is also the question of impetus. While the Fordney-McCumber Tariff Act of 1922 has been attributed to the recession of 1921, the Smoot-Hawley Tariff Act of 1930, originally drafted November 1928, has no such impetus. The U.S. economy in late 1928, early 1929 was at its zenith, its stock market climbing to dizzying heights (roaring twenties).

Clearly, new leads are needed, new hypotheses formulated. This book is an attempt at understanding U.S. tariff legislation in the early 20th century, a time when the United States had assumed the lead of the Western industrialized world. Drawing on earlier work on electrification, mass production, the Stock Market Crash of 1929 and the Great Depression (Beaudreau 1996), we argue that Smoot-Hawley Tariff Act of 1930, like the Repeal of the Corn Laws in Britain in 1846, was a policy response to the problem of underincome—that is, the inability of private, wage and price-setting Nash economies to move to the higher equilibrium growth path defined by the new technology. The electrification of the U.S. economy in the 1910s and 1920s increased productivity by roughly 40 percent. Nominal and real income, however, failed to increase commensurately, with the result that U.S. companies produced significantly below capacity.

As it turned out, tariff legislation in the 1920s was less about traditional import substitution (Henry Clay's *American System*, John A. Macdonald's *National Policy*), as it was about nudging the U.S. economy closer to its new-found potential. Unfortunately, the latter required the former, which explains the confusion surrounding the tariff act. The evidence, we submit, is overwhelming. Consider, for example, the following remarks made by Senator Smoot in the Senate, in response to claims by Democrats that unemployment was on the rise in 1927 and 1928.

> Senator Smoot insisted that the picture drawn by the Democrats on Monday, when the Senate passed the Senate resolution, was much overdrawn. He admitted that some unemployment existed, but insisted that it did not compare with that of 1920 and 1921 when the Republicans came into power after eight years of Democratic administration. As for one reason for a degree of unemployment, Senator Smoot referred to large importations of foreign merchandise that have been steadily reaching American shores in spite of the Republican protective tariff.... These imports have a tendency to supplant large quantities of American goods, despite the tariff, thus slowing down many American industries. There also was an over-supply or over-production in many lines, Senator Smoot contended, and over-production or under-consumption in the textiles industries.[1]
>
> A slow-down of many industries helps to increase industrial unemployment, and the result is immediately felt in the lowering of the consuming power of the wage earners. This has brought about what may be called an oversupply or overproduction existing in many lines; and we might add that mass production has cut a great figure in the amount of production in the United States in special lines.[2]

According to Senator Smoot, the U.S. economy, in early 1928, was characterized by oversupply, the chief culprits being higher imports and mass production. Why mass production should lead to conditions of generalized oversupply is not clear from his remarks. After all, according to *Say's Law*, the accepted orthodoxy at the time, supply creates its own demand, thus ruling out generalized oversupply.

Years later, Senator Smoot offered a number of reasons, including the destruction of life and property in World War I, and the failure to adjust purchasing power to productive capacity.

> On his return to Utah in August 1932, in preparation for his final battle in political life, Smoot advised his people that it had been the common attitude in 1930 to attributed the depression to unwise governmental policies, with the Smoot-Hawley act specified. Lest there were some obsessed with heresy, he declared, "To hold the American tariff policy, or any other policy of our government, responsible for this gigantic deflationary move is only

to display one's ignorance of its sweeping universal character." He found that "The world is paying for its ruthless destruction of life and property in the World War and for its failure to adjust purchasing power to productive capacity during the industrial revolution of the decade following the war." (Merrill 1990, 340)

The book is organized as follows. Chapter 1 presents a survey of U.S. tariff policy with an emphasis on the late 19th century/early 20th century. This is followed by Chapter 2 which presents a post-Walrasian model of producer-merchant exchange. Specifically, we begin with a review of the literature on money and exchange, paying particular attention to exchange technologies. That is, the means by which goods and services are exchanged (e.g. barter, money, intermediated, and non intermediated trade). This provides a convenient segue into the model proper. The problem of underincome is then identified and analyzed in the context of technological change, specifically of the electrification of U.S. industry. The results of this chapter constitute the analytical framework used in Chapters 3 to 7 where the many facets of the Smoot-Hawley Tariff Act are examined. Chapter 3 examines the technology shock that was the electrification of U.S. industry, focusing particular attention on the developments at the Ford Motor Company and the fallout for U.S. manufacturing as a whole, including the problem of underincome and its dual, the problem of excess capacity. This sets the stage for the in-depth analysis of the first policy response, namely the Smoot-Hawley Tariff Bill, that follows. Particular attention is focused on the debate in the Senate, where opposing views of both the problem and the proposed solution collided. Failure to push the tariff bill though the Senate, owing in large measure to thirteen "Insurgent Republicans," was extremely consequential. Chief among these was the effect on investor expectations. The scheduled high tariffs on manufactures had buoyed earnings expectations. U.S. firms' market shares would increase at the expense of foreign competitors, thus closing the widening gap between actual and potential output. Capacity would, as such, be reached without raising wages as Henry Ford and others recommended.

News of the imminent failure of the Smoot-Hawley Tariff Bill to pass in the Senate sent stock market prices spiraling downward, back to their pre-tariff bill level. With hope gone, companies revised downwards investment in new equipment, the end result of which was the Great Depression. Herbert Hoover's electoral defeat in 1932 marked a watershed of sorts, especially regarding the underlying problem of underincome. Smoot, Grundy, and others had attempted naively to solve the problem using the Republican Party all-purpose policy instrument, namely tariff revisions. The new administration (i.e. Roosevelt) focused its attention on the underlying coordination failure. Taking its cues from the likes of Rexford G. Tugwell, Alfred Berle, and Robert F. Wagner, the Roosevelt Administration set out to reform the very nature of capitalism. Seeing the problem in terms of a Schelling-type coordination game (wages and prices), they drafted the National Industrial Recovery Act, the purpose of which was to provide a framework in which to resolve the corresponding coordination failures. Chapter 6 examines the NIRA and the NRA using the theoretical results derived in Chapter 2. Chapter 7 examines the wisdom of commercial policy as a policy instrument in the presence of underincome. Estimates of the technology shock and output gap are provided. When juxtaposed against trade data, specifically, import data, these estimates raise doubt on the efficacy of commercial policy, specifically on the efficacy of the Smoot-Hawley Tariff Bill in periods of paradigm technological change.

As shall be argued, the two policy responses to the problem of underincome occasioned by the electrification of U.S. industry were complementary, if only in their objectives: both sought to close the widening gap between actual and potential output via government policy. In fact, one could argue that the NIRA and the accompanying National Recovery Administration (NRA), constitute corroborative evidence of the underincome theory of the Smoot-Hawley Tariff Act outlined in Beaudreau (1996) and developed in greater detail here.

1

U.S. Tariff Policy: A General Purpose Instrument

The initial policy and the groundwork of the enlightened universe is protection. The civilized world has grown out and away from barbaric free trade, and has developed a very universal recognition of the protective idea. In the savage state everything connected with human existence bears the impress of free trade and an unlimited and uncontrolled personal license. That condition allows the absolute equality and freedom of the individual, restrained alone by the physical strength and power of his fellow-savages.

To him belongs everything, provided he can take and hold everything. His motto is "The world is mine," modified only by the limit of his physical ability. Out of the condition of savage freedom, and through the various stages of development and enlightenment time as brought into existence the family, the home, the society, the State, and the nation.

And with this development and enlightenment the proper status of the individual became apparent. The preservation of his rights and the definition of his duties demanded the establishment of the rules of society and the laws of civilized countries. The policy of union and cooperation in maintenance of law has become a fixed element in all modern govern-

ments. The people join together for mutual protection, and so joined together in societies, in municipal bodies, or in nations, they bear mutual burdens in order that they bear mutual benefits.

They waive a certain portion of their individual, natural rights, and the prerogatives which adhere to him in a savage state, that they may enjoy the mutual protection guaranteed by the government which they have established. They are joined in government establishment, as citizens of the same, and they owe their allegiance to that establishment in return for the protection it gives them. Violation of this allegiance is treason to the state.

—*Senator Cullon*, Senate Congressional Record

The economic, political and social history of the United States of America is intimately tied to trade, specifically to trade developments both abroad and at home. In fact, one could argue that trade runs through the core of the American experience. The very existence of a number of the original thirteen colonies owes to trade, specifically to chartered trading companies. The birth of the nation (i.e. the war of independence) owed to trade concerns, namely to tariffs and taxes and to rivalry among merchants (British and American). With the end of hostilities in Europe (post-War of 1812), the new confederacy turned its attention to internal trade, erecting a virtual tariff wall around the country, one whose height increased progressively over the course of the 19th and early 20th centuries. Attempts by a number of administrations to lower tariffs were often unsuccessful, and when successful, were typically revoked by subsequent administrations.

This left an indelible mark on the nation, on its character, and on its institutions. For example, unlike other nation states, government in the United States was financed almost exclusively by tariff revenue—that is, from revenue generated by external trade. Head taxes and *imposts* were prohibited by the *Articles of Confederation*, and ultimately by the U.S. constitution. As bold a break with what at the time was the norm could only have been attempted in what was a highly open economy. Trade was the lifeline of the new confederation, economically, financially, and culturally. Independence did not spell the end of trade.

In this chapter, we examine the history of U.S. tariff policy, from the pre-Revolutionary War period to the early 20th century. However, unlike previous work which was based largely on conventional trade theory (gains from trade, tariffs as welfare reducing), we opt to examine it through four analytical prisms, namely (*i*) communication and coordination strategies, (*ii*) industrial policy, (iii) revenue tool, and (*iv*) macroeconomic policy.

Tariff Theory

U.S. tariff policy has, for the most part, been studied within the context of classical political economy. Accordingly, tariffs, by distorting relative prices, reduce the gains from trade, and, as such, are welfare reducing. Anything short of free, unimpeded trade is Pareto dominated. It goes without saying that, seen through this prism, U.S. trade policy was, for over a century and a half, misguided, misdirected, mistaken, and "just plain wrong." Legislators from Thomas Jefferson to Alexander Hamilton to Reed Smoot systematically sabotaged overall welfare, the cost of which is incalculable.

To make such allegations, we argue, is to not understand, nor appreciate the subtleties, and, indeed, the many facets of tariffs and tariff policy. To make such allegations is to ignore important aspects of tariff policy in the United States, and indeed, throughout the Western hemisphere. To make such allegations is to condone Ricardian trade theory, something most American legislators openly and repeatedly refused to do throughout most of the 19th century and early 20th century.

Tariffs, as the American experience clearly demonstrates, were called upon to achieve a number of objectives, including raising government revenue, altering industry structure, and Keynesian-style beggar-thy-neighbor policies. In this section, we examine each of these, from the point of view of government, industry structure, and full employment.

The early history of tariffs is intimately tied to the rise of large-scale specialization and exchange. As pointed out in Beaudreau (2004), large-scale specialization and exchange, and government—temples and priests—went hand-in-hand. The latter provided the institutional framework for large-scale specialization and exchange. Trade as such relied on government, more specifically, on the government's ability to create markets, itself the result of its ability to raise revenue (to purchase public goods). With citizenship came access to the "market," as well as the obligation to pay one's "fair" share, in the form of taxation. In many cultures, such payments are still referred to as tariffs. A tariff is, as such, the cost of government services. In short, large-scale specialization and exchange is not a spontaneous activity, but rather is costly, the costs of which are defrayed by the citizenship.

This raises the question of the exchange involving non-citizens, specifically, how will they be treated, and under what conditions? As large-scale specialization and exchange (markets) is a public good, it follows that the non-citizen is the classic free-rider, taking advantage of the opportunities provided by the market, but not paying. This led to the levying of tariffs on foreign trade. Tariffs, as such, were not intended to discourage trade *per se*, but to internalize what would otherwise be an externality. The more open is an economy, the greater is the proportion of government revenue raised from tariffs on foreign trade to overall revenue.

Seen in this light, tariffs are welfare increasing. Without tariffs, and indeed, without taxes and tariffs, markets would simply not exist, the consequences of which are enormous. Such a view is implicit in Republican Senator Cullon's remarks in the U.S. Senate in the debate leading up to the Dingley Tariff Act:

> The initial policy and the groundwork of the enlightened universe is protection. The civilized world has grown out and away from barbaric free trade, and has developed a very universal recognition of the protective idea. In the savage state everything connected with human existence bears the impress of free trade and an unlimited and uncontrolled personal license. That condition allows the absolute equality and freedom of the individual, restrained alone by the physical strength and power of his fellow-savages.
>
> To him belongs everything, provided he can take and hold everything. His motto is "The world is mine," modified only by the limit of his physical ability. Out of the condition of savage freedom, and through the various stages of development and enlightenment time as brought into existence the family, the home, the society, the State, and the nation.
>
> And with this development and enlightenment the proper status of the individual became apparent. The preservation of his rights and the definition of his duties demanded the establishment of the rules of society and the laws of civilized countries. The policy of union and cooperation in maintenance of law has become a fixed element in all modern governments. The people join together for mutual protection, and so joined together in societies, in municipal bodies, or in nations, they bear mutual burdens in order that they bear mutual benefits.
>
> They waive a certain portion of their individual, natural rights, and the prerogatives which adhere to him in a savage state, that they may enjoy the mutual protection guaranteed by the government which they have established. They are joined in government establishment, as citizens of the same, and they owe their allegiance to that establishment in return for the

protection it gives them. Violation of this allegiance is treason to the state. (*Senate Congressional Record*, April 27, 1894, 4166)

Seen in this light, tariffs are not discriminatory. Non-citizens (foreigners) that want to trade in the corresponding "trade network" have to pay what is essentially a user-fee. Where it becomes discriminatory, however, is when they *de facto* pay twice, once at home, and once abroad. Reciprocal free trade eliminates what is essentially double taxation.

Taxation, Tariffs and Markets in the Pre-Revolutionary America

This view of taxation, tariffs and markets provides a convenient framework to understand pre-revolutionary America. Like other nation-states in the 17th century, Great Britain financed its activities by various forms of taxation, direct and indirect. Joint-stock trading companies were obliged to remit a portion of their profits to the Crown. A good example of this is the British East India Company. Citizens contributed to financing government via a series of tariffs and taxes levied on various goods. The proceeds were used to finance government.

In the case of the Thirteen colonies, were all trade to have been conducted by say the British East India Company, there would have been no need for tariffs and taxes. Prices would have been adjusted in such a way so as to reflect the cost of making markets (trade networks). As it turned out, for much of the 17th century, the British government financed most of its activities with levies on chartered, joint-stock companies. It is important to note that the resulting system of colonial trade worked, in the sense that it provided gains from trade for all parties concerned. The Thirteen colonies and Great Britain took profit from mercantilism.

A number of developments, however, marred what was otherwise a highly complex and successful trading arrangement. The first was the emergence of colonial merchants who, like their British counterparts, were skilled at trading within the British empire. In other words, not all trade was conducted by and for British merchants. The second was the Molasses Act of 1733 which attempted to stem the growing tide of imported molasses from the Dutch and French West Indies. Increasingly, colonial merchants were importing molasses and turning it into rum in Massachusetts and Rhode Island. This prompted an increase in smuggling and contraband, the result of which was to reduce the Crown's revenue. Throughout much of this period, extra-empire trade, most of it illegal, increased manifold, thus diminishing the Crown's revenue base.

The third development was the imperial wars of the late 17th century/early 18th century, which, as wars are wont to do, put a strain on public finances. The costliest of these was the Seven Years War with France and Spain. While victorious, Britain was straddled with an enormous debt. Looking to defray the costs of the war, it sought new measures to tap into the wealth of the Thirteen colonies. Given the presence of smuggling and extra-empire trade, it resorted to direct taxation in the form of the Sugar Act of 1764, the Stamp Act of 1765, and the Townsend Act of 1767.

While perceived of, on the part of the colonists as excessive, the Crown had no choice but to opt for direct taxation, given (*i*) increasing contraband and extra-empire trade by colonial merchants, and (*ii*) the outstanding war debt. Put differently, empires, especially expanding ones, are expensive propositions. With the annexation of New France and the Ohio Valley (the Quebec Act of 1774), British North America offered unparalleled trading opportunities. These opportunities, however, were not costless.

The rest, as they say, is history. In little time, the Crown's attempt at reeling in the free-riding colony was met with open hostility, which, in time, degenerated into open conflict, revolt, and finally independence. Each of the Thirteen colonies became independent republics, which, for the purposes of defense, joined in a loose confederacy known as the United States of America.

Taxation, Tariffs and Markets in the Post-Revolutionary America

Like all other nation-states, the thirteen newly-minted republics had to raise revenue with which to defray the overall cost of government. Shedding the yoke of colonial rule did not, unfortunately, do away with government and all things governmental. Each state had the obligation to provide services to its citizens, services that they had become accustomed to under British rule.

In most instances, states opted for indirect taxation, specifically of trade. As each had the constitutional right to levy taxes and tariffs, indirect taxation was the chief revenue instrument. In many regards, each state behaved in a manner not unlike Great Britain prior to the Revolution War, the one important difference being representation—that is, taxation with representation.

In this period, trade with Britain continued, as did trade with continental Europe and the West and East Indies. American merchants plied the waterways of the world, in search of arbitrage opportunities. John Jacob Astor is a case in point.

Their acumen had not gone unnoticed in Great Britain which throughout this period kept a watchful eye on developments in the port cities of the eastern seaboard. Rising hostilities in northern Europe, particularly those involving Great Britain and France, proved to be a watershed for American merchants who assumed most of the carrying trade between southern Europe and the West Indies.

With the end of the hostilities in Europe came a lull in trade. Moreover, with the rise of Great Britain as "the" leading manufacturing nation in the world, America's future appeared grim. Whereas U.S. merchants had, until then, fared relatively well on world markets, their days were numbered. Britain insisted on controlling trade in manufactures. This had dire consequences for U.S. merchants. In little time, British merchants, offering cheaper wares, would crowd out their American counterparts. This was to have dire consequences for the young confederation. The fallout divided the United States, with the fault line running east to west. Northern merchants, based in the port cities (Boston, New York), pressed the government to impose tariffs on manufactures, thus favoring import substitution and fostering industry. This stood in contrast with the South, where exports of staples (e.g. food and cotton) to Great Britain continued to increase. Throughout this period, Southern merchants strengthened their ties with Great Britain. With the demand for feedstocks in Great Britain growing at a "torrid" pace, the future looked particularly promising. This raised a number of questions, notably could Southern merchants deliver? Could they provide the required feedstocks?

Thus was born the fundamental antagonism of the 19th century, one pitting two sets of merchants, those from the North, and those from the South, the former having been crowded out of the carrying trade by British merchants, and the latter having been drawn into the British fold. This antagonism was to play itself out on many fronts, from the cost of labor (slavery) to tariff policy. Northerners advocated high external tariffs for obvious reasons, while Southerners favored free trade. Northerners, wanting to divert Southern staples away from Great Britain, and over to their factories, embarked on a course of action, the likes of which contributed directly to the Civil War in 1861. Evidence of the commercial underpinnings of the conflict is provided by the following excerpt from Jefferson Davis' Inaugural Speech, delivered on Monday, April 15, 1861 in the Capital.

> An agricultural people, whose chief interest is the export of a commodity required in every manufacturing country, our true policy is peace and the freest trade which our necessities will permit. It is alike our interest, and that of all those to whom we would sell and from whom we would buy, that there should be fewest practicable restrictions upon the interchange of commodities. There can be but little rivalry between ours and any manufacturing or navigating community, such as the northeastern States of the American Union. It must follow, therefore, that a mutual interest would invite good will and kind offices. If, however, passion or the lust of dominion should cloud the judgment or inflame the ambition of those States, we must prepare to meet the emergency, and to maintain, by the final arbitrament of the sword, the position which we have assumed among the nations of the earth. We have entered upon the career of independence, and it must be inflexibly pursued. Through many years of controversy with our late associates, the Northern States, we have vainly endeavored to secure tranquility, and to obtain respect for the rights to which we are entitled. As a necessity, not a choice, we have resorted to the remedy of separation; and henceforth our energies must be directed to the conduct of our own affairs, and the perpetuity of the Confederacy which we have formed. If a just perception of mutual interest shall permit us peaceably to pursue our separate political career, my most earnest desire will have been fulfilled; but if this be denied to us, and the integrity of our territory and jurisdiction be assailed it, it will but remain for us, with firm resolve, to appeal to arms and invoke the blessings of Providence on a just cause.

From the end of the War of 1812 to the 1860s, tariffs had performed admirably well, providing revenue to the U.S. treasury and keeping British manufactures at bay. The North had embarked on a path of industrialization known as the American System, while the South had prospered as a source of staples for both the North and Europe, especially Great Britain. Tariffs were an important source of revenue for the U.S. treasury. Direct taxation, in keeping with the original *Articles of Confederation*, was kept at a minimum.

Throughout the ensuing decades, tariff policy evolved in response to these two objectives, namely import substitution and revenue. All of this changed with the coming of the second industrial revolution. As had been the case with Great Britain's experience with steam power, the massive energy-based increase in productive capacity that resulted from the electrification of material processes opened up a veritable chasm between actual and potential output, between actual income and potential income, and between actual and potential expenditure. The British chose free trade as a means of closing the gap; the U.S. opted for the obverse: higher tariffs as a means to secure a larger share of the domestic market for its firms. As had been the case in the early 19th century, higher tariffs would crowd out foreign merchants and goods, thus closing the chasm between actual and potential output. Chapter 4 chronicles the evolution of U.S. tariff policy from its early incarnation as a revenue and industrial structure tool, to that of an instrument of macroeconomic policy.

The Four Periods of U.S. Tariff Policy

The history of U.S. tariff policy can be broken down into four distinct periods, namely (*I*) from 1789 to 1817, (*II*) from 1817 to 1890, (*III*) from 1890 to 1934, and (*IV*) from 1934 to the present (see Table 1.1). The first period, from 1789 to 1817, is characterized by revenue considerations. As the *Articles of Confederation* interdicted direct taxation, revenue sources would be needed. One such source was a tax on imports. The purpose, however, is not to discourage trade, nor to protect domestic manufacturers. Remember that War of Independence did not put an end to the carrying trade with Great Britain, and indeed with the rest of the world. In fact, in this period, the U.S. benefited from unrest and conflict in Europe to increase its role in world trade. The second period begins with the end of hostilities in Europe and the emergence of Great Britain as the dominant manufacturing nation in the world. Under the articles of the Navigation Act, British vessels and only British vessels could carry British products, which effectively put an end to U.S. mercantile interests. Having been squeezed out, U.S. merchants turned their attention to import substitution, the end result of which was the "American System" which was founded on high external tariffs. From 1817 to 1890, the latter date corresponding to the McKinley Tariff Act of 1890, U.S. tariff policy was founded on import substitution—specifically on substituting U.S. products for British products. The third period 1890-1934 coincides with the start of the second industrial revolution. More productive than ever, U.S. manufacturers look to tariff policy as a means of increasing sales, revenue, earnings and ultimately, profits. The fourth period 1934 to the present marks the coming of age of U.S. industry. No longer a second or third-rate nation, the U.S. sits atop the world economy. Its firms are multinational in scope, having branch plants on all continents and in virtually every country.

Table 1.1
Tariff Periods, Tariff Changes and Tariff Rates
1789-1974 [*]

Period	Year	Tariff	All	Dutiable
I	1789	First tariff (average duty about 9%)		
I	1812	Doubling of duties for war		
II	1816	Postwar protection of cotton goods, iron, paper, and glass	43	45
II	1824	Conflict of sectional interests	47	50
II	1828	"Tariff of abominations"	44	48
II	1832	Some reductions; nullification	39	43
II	1833	Clay's compromise; reduction to 20% by 1842	29	38
II	1842	"Black tariff," increased protection	19	26
II	1846	Walker Tariff; moderate and simplified	29	34
II	1854	Elgin-Marcy Treaty, Canadian reciprocity	24	26
II	1857	Further reductions	19	22
II	1861	Morill Tariff, return to high rates	14	19
II	1865	Wartime increases, compensation for internal taxes	28	34
II	1872	10 percent cut in protective rates	38	42
II	1875	Reversal of 1872 reduction	29	41
II	1883	Mixed changes, largely protectionist	30	43
III	1890	McKinley Tariff, extension of protection	30	45
III	1894	Wilson-Gorman Tariff, some reductions; income tax	21	50
III	1897	Dingley Tariff; return to many 1890 rates	22	42
III	1909	Payne-Aldrich Tariff, the "true principle"	23	43
III	1911	Reciprocity with Canada (failed)	20	41
III	1913	Underwood Tariff, a "competitive tariff"; income tax	18	40

Table 1.1
Tariff Periods, Tariff Changes and Tariff Rates
1789-1974 (Continued)[*]

III	1921	Emergency Tariff Act, high agricultural duties	11	29
III	1922	Fordney-McCumber Tariff, chemicals and metallurgical products	15	38
III	1930	Hawley-Smoot Tariff	15	45
IV	1934	Reciprocal Trade Agreements Act, reductions up to 50%	18	47
IV	1945	Trade Agreements Extension Act, a further 50% reduction	9	28
IV	1947	General Agreement on Tariffs and Trade (GATT)	8	19
IV	1955	Stronger "escape" clause	5	12
IV	1958	Stronger "escape" and "national security" clauses	6	11
IV	1962	Trade Expansion Act, a further 50% reduction, and adjustment assistance	8	12
IV	1964	Kennedy Round, voluntary restraints	7	12
IV	1971	Temporary import surcharge	6	9
IV	1974	Trade Act, 60% reductions allowed, multinational trade negotiations begun	4	8
IV	1976	Elimination of many duties on Third World Products	4	6

[*]   Source: U.S. Department of Commerce (1975).

Conclusions

As we have attempted to show, tariffs played a key role in U.S. economic history, from the early 17th century to the present. Over the course of this period, they were called upon to perform a number of tasks from raising revenue, to developing an industrial base, to raising capacity utilization rates in the presence of technology shocks, to signalling a new era of free trade, earning tariff policy the nmenonic of general purpose policy instrument.

The Smoot-Hawley Tariff Act falls into the third category, namely being an instrument of raising capacity utilization rates in the presence of what is perhaps the greatest technology shock of the modern era, namely electrification (the Second Industrial Revolution). The next chapter develops the theory of underincome, which will be used in subsequent chapters to chronicle and analyze U.S. tariff policy in the late 1920s (*Period III*).

2

The Theory of Underincome

We've got to stop that gouging process if we want to see all of the people reasonably prosperous. There is only one rule for industrialists and that is: Make the best quality of goods possible at the lowest cost paying the highest wages possible. Nothing can be right in this country until wages are right. The life of business comes forth from the people in orders. The factories are not stopped for lack of money but for lack of orders. Money loaned at the top means nothing. Money spent at the bottom starts everything. we think that if industrial leaders had been willing to push wages up and up during the last thirty years the present economic ills would at least not be as great as they are. If the government can help in these matters, well and good, but the government has not a rosy record in running itself thus far.

—Henry Ford

Introduction

The problem of underincome is, first and foremost, an exchange-related problem, one that is inexorably linked to the nature of the Schelling-type coordination game played by producers and merchants. Specifically, aggregate income, whether nominal or real, fails to increase commensurately with society's ability to produce output, heretofore referred to as potential productive capacity, or simply productive capacity. Producers have no private incentives to increase wages, which, combined with the fact that profits are a residual form of income paid out only when output has been delivered to merchants, results in income inertia, or simply, underincome.

This chapter outlines a post-Walrasian theory of underincome. To this end, a parsimonious model of producer-merchant exchange is developed. Finding existing models of exchange (monetary, neo-Walrasian) to be incomplete, we, following in the footsteps of 19th-century Swedish economist Knut Wicksell, develop a producer-merchant model of exchange. We assume the existence of two sets of market coordinating agents, producers and merchants. The former coordinate production in factor markets, while the latter coordinate exchange in product markets. Both finance their transactions using costless bank trade credit.

Money and Exchange

It could be argued that money and its role in the exchange process is one of the oldest—indeed, the oldest—topic in economics, going as far back in time as the 16th century, when monks at the Universidad de Salamanca in Salamanca, Spain, examined the problem of species-induced inflation. Recent discoveries of gold in the New World ushered in decades of price inflation in the Iberian peninsula. This was followed by Jean Bodin's work on inflation in 17th-century France, and David Hume's work in the early 18th century. Add to this John Law's 1705 controversial work on the nature of money and wealth.

Unfortunately, interest in all things monetary waned for the most part in the late 18th and 19th centuries. Classical and neoclassical political economy was cast in real terms. Monetary issues were, for the most part, an afterthought. Witness, for example, the classical dichotomy that divorced real from monetary issues (i.e. classical dichotomy). Money, it was argued, was, at best, a veil.

The resulting void and the breakdown of the gold standard in the early 20th century rekindled interest in money and related matters. Prompted by the breakdown of the gold standard in World War I, John Maynard Keynes, Gustav Cassel, and Irving Fisher began reexamining the role of money in the economy. The result was a series of theoretical developments that today constitute the core of monetary economics. These include the precautionary demand for money, the speculative demand for money, and price indexes, to name just a few. These early contributions were followed, in the post-World War II period, by numerous attempts at modelling a monetary economy, beginning with Don Patinkin's *Money, Interest and Prices* in 1958. In spite of these contributions, little was known of the so-called nuts and bolts of money and exchange. For example, most-if not all—of the models abstracted, for the most part, from production activity, the focus being on pure-exchange economies.

The Problem of Exchange

It is generally argued that the main economic problem is scarcity, defined as unlimited needs/desires in the face of limited resources. Microeconomics and macroeconomics examine the problem of resource allocation, itself founded on the problem of scarcity. Exchange, the process whereby goods and factor inputs are traded, is assumed to be frictionless, and hence, a non-issue (e.g. *The Classical Dichotomy*). For example, once output (value added, transformation, goods and services) is produced, it is assumed that its dual, money income, exists, and that, eventually, it will be spent (consumed or invested). Markets are assumed to exist, and, moreover, constitute a sufficient condition for exchange.

In this chapter, and, indeed, throughout this book, we take the opposite view, namely that exchange and the exchange process have, are, and will undoubtedly continue to rank among the most important problems in western industrialized—and indeed, pre-industrialized—countries. Traditionally-defined resource allocation (production, distribution, and expenditure), consequently, is a second-order problem. The pitfalls of the first industrial revolution (recessions, depressions, a falling standard of living), we argue, were exchange related, specifically were the result of underincome. As pointed out earlier, underincome refers to the inability of private, Nash economies—of which the British economy in the early 19th century is the defining example—to generate income commensurately with productive capacity (Beaudreau 1999). The Great Depression in the 1930s was the result of underincome (Beaudreau 1996,1999). We begin by examining exchange and the exchange process as currently modelled in economics.

THE SCIENCE OF EXCHANGE

How is exchange formalized in economics? How is it modelled? What is the relevant time framework? Who are the relevant agents? What are the relevant institutions? Surprisingly, microeconomics and macroeconomics, for the most part, have ignored and continue to ignore these questions. Implicit in introductory microeconomics and macroeconomics is the view that once value added (output) is produced, it is costlessly exchanged, and then consumed and/or invested.

This view is formalized in terms of the "circular flow" diagram of economic activity, where the exchange process is likened to a highway with goods and services going in one direction and money going in the other. There is no beginning and no end. Moreover, the highway is assumed to exist. There is no mention of its architects, its builders, and its maintainers. Goods and money spontaneously flow in opposite directions. In short, the classical dichotomy.

While useful as an overview of economic activity as a whole, it stops short of providing an empirically-consistent model of the origins of economic activity (i.e. Adam Smith's notion of our innate propensity to "truck and barter"). Missing are the agents who make production and trade possible, namely producers, merchants, and bankers, the first coordinating production activity, the second coordinating trade activity, and the third providing the wherewithal for both, namely credit (trade credit)—what Williford King referred to as "bank credit." Producers coordinate production in a market setting, buying factor inputs, and selling the final product to merchants. The latter coordinate distribution, purchasing goods from producers, and selling them to the consuming public. This raises the question, why are merchants and bankers, as essential to trade as producers, virtually absent from mainstream political economy?

This is an interesting question, one that, unfortunately, extends well beyond the scope of this book. Suffice it to say that in the last century, a number of political economists have attempted to model exchange scientifically—that is, with an eye to the real world. One such attempt was that of Swedish political economist Knut Wicksell, who in *Interest and Prices*, published in 1898, presented a sequential model of exchange involving bankers, producers and merchants.

> We may assume further that production begins everywhere at the same moment of time, at the beginning of the economic year, which need not, of course, coincide with the calendar year; and we may assume that the final product, the consumption goods, are not completed or available for exchange until the end of the year. This would correspond in some ways to the situation of former times, when in many districts the exchange of commodities was concentrated on one, or a few, great annual markets.
>
> The total quantity of consumption goods is then the same thing as the quantity of liquid real capital in its free form; or rather it is the same thing as the quantity of this capital, inclusive of the amount with which the owners of capital have the right annually to credit themselves as remuneration

for the capital employed in the previous year and which they consume on their own account during the current year.

Our imaginary procedure is then as follows: At the beginning of the year the entrepreneurs borrow their capital from the banks, in the form of a sum of money K. This is equal to the value of the total amount of available real capital, that is to say, of the total amount of consumption goods completed during the previous years minus the interest drawn in the previous year by the capitalist. This money capital is now paid to the workers and to the landlords; and at the same time entrepreneurs allocate to themselves an amount as remuneration for their own labour, risk-taking, etc., and pay the normal competitive rents for such

"rent-earning goods" (sites, buildings, machines) as may be in their possession. With the aid of this money, the whole of the available commodity capital is now bought up by the consumers and the, and the money capital K returns once again to the banks in the shape of the deposits made by the capitalist dealers. The goods are completed only at the end of the economic year, and it is only then that the entrepreneurs can meet their liabilities. It follows that the credit that is granted by the banks to the entrepreneurs partakes of the character of one-year loans. (Wicksell 1898, 139)

Others who attempted empirically-consistent (i.e. more realistic) models of exchange in industrial economies include Clifford H. Douglas, the founder of the Social Credit movement. Consider the following passages taken from Douglas' *Monopoly of Credit*.

Let us imagine a capitalist to own a certain piece of land, on which is a house, and a building containing the necessary machinery for preparing, spinning, and weaving linen, and that the land is capable of growing in addition to the flax, all the food necessary to maintain a man. Let us further imagine that the capitalist in the first place allows a man to live free of all payment in the house and to have the use of all the foodstuffs that he grows on condition that he also grows, spins and weaves a certain amount of linen for the capitalist. Let us further imagine that after a time, this arrangement is altered by the payment to the man of £1 a week for the work on the linen business, but that this £1 is taken back each week as rent for the house and payment for the foodstuffs.

Let us now imagine that from the time the flax is picked to the time the linen is delivered to the capitalist, a period of six weeks elapses. Obviously, the cost of the linen must be £6, and this will be the price, plus profit, which the capitalist would place on it. Quite obviously only one-sixth of the purchasing power necessary to buy linen is now available, although "at some time or other," all £6 has been distributed.

Let us now imagine that half of the employee's time is devoted to making a machine which will do all the work of preparing and manufacturing linen, and that the manufacture of this machine takes twelve weeks. We may therefore say that the machine costs £6, the total value of the production of the machine and the flax being still £1 per week. At the end of the period, the machine is substituted for the man, the machine being driven, we suppose, by the burning of the food which was previously consumed by the man, and the machine being housed in the house previously occupied by the man, and being automatic. The capitalist would be justified in saying that the cost of operation of the machine is £1, per week as before, and if there is any wear, he will also be justified in allocating the cost of this wear to the cost of linen. It should be noticed, however that he will now not distribute any money at all, since it is obviously no use offering a £1 note a week to a machine. (Douglas 1951, 40)

In the modern industrial system, this process can be identified easily in the form of machine charges. For instance, a modern stamping plant may require to add 600 per cent to its labour charges to cover its machine charges. This sum not being in any true sense profit. In such a case, for every £1 expended in a given period in wages, £6 making £7 in all, would be carried forward into prices. Although this is an extreme case, the constant, and in one sense desirable, tendency is for direct charges to increase as a result of the replacement of human labor by machinery. There is no difference between a plant charge of this nature and a similar sum repaid as a "B" payment. (Douglas 1951, 42)

Clearly, Wicksell and Douglas were the exceptions. Classical, radical, neoclassical, Keynesian, New-Keynesian and New-Classical political economists ignored the underlying mechanics of exchange. The absence of empirically-consistent models of exchange, we maintain, owes, in large part, to the nature and intent of classical political economy. By the late 18th century, mercantilism was firmly entrenched in most European capitals. Among other things, mercantilism equated money with wealth. The more money (specie) a country had, the wealthier it was. The first to disagree were the French Physiocrats, according to whom, only land was capable of producing wealth. This was followed by the classical political economists in Great Britain (e.g. Adam Smith and David Ricardo), who saw large-scale manufacturing, made possible by the Watt-Boulton reciprocating steam engine, as the ultimate source of wealth.

The resulting enmity, we argue, had a profound effect on political economy. Money, and, more importantly, the exchange process itself, were, in the ensuing period, virtually ignored. Economic principles were theretofore cast in real terms. Real prices (exchange ratios) were preferred to nominal prices (prices in terms of money) (Ricardo 1817). This aversion to all things monetary extended well into the 20th century, as evidenced by the presence of the classical dichotomy, which separated the real sector from the monetary sector (Pigou 1917,1949; Hicks 1935). Arthur Pigou explains:

> In the years preceding the First World War there were in common use among economists a number of metaphors, all of a like general tendency, about the role of money. 'Money is a wrapper in which goods come to you'; 'money is the garment draped round the body of economic life'; 'money is a veil behind which the action of real economic forces is concealed'. The mercantilists, it was said, in their blindness, mistook money for wealth; we must not do that. We must strip the garment, tear away the veil, and look through the thing to the thing signified. (Pigou 1949, 18)

The Great Depression and the writings of John M. Keynes ushered in a new era. Suddenly, money took on a whole new meaning. The problem, however, was that it had been ignored for over a century and a half. To Keynes, the depression in the mid-1920s in Great Britain was first and foremost a monetary phenomenon, specifically, the result of an overvalued currency (i.e. the British Pound) and an inflated bank rate (Beaudreau 1999b). The problem, however, was the absence of formal models incorporating money (Clower and Howitt 2000).

In the post-World War II period, attempts were made to fill this void. Don Patinkin's *Money, Interest and Prices*, for example, was first published in 1950, followed by a series of critiques, beginning with Chris Archibald and Richard Lipsey's 1958 paper "Monetary and Value Theory: A Critique of Lange and Patinkin," followed by Robert Clower's seminal paper, "The Keynesian Counter-Revolution: A Theoretical Appraisal." published in 1967. The problems were numerous. Among the most serious was the Clower critique, namely that in Patinkin's model, monetary exchange was altogether absent. Money entered the representative agent's utility function much like any other good. To Clower, money was synonymous with exchange. A good theory of money would, as such, require a good theory of exchange. This, as it turns out, is where the literature is today. Robert Clower continues to this day to search for the "holy grail" of monetary theory, namely a unified theory of money and markets (Clower and Howitt 2000; Clower 1995).

Like the literature it sought to replace, this body of work suffers from a number of shortcomings. One is its ahistorical nature. No attempt was (is) made to trace the development of money and markets. Instead, like Patinkin, money and markets are modelled in a setting in which agents are assumed to have specialized, and, secondly, are agglomerated geographically (Howitt 1998). In other words, trade, markets and money are not derived from first principles, namely, spatially-dispersed autarkic agents (groupings of agents). Instead, starting with geographically-agglomerated, specialized agents, the development of markets is examined, or, more accurately, imagined (Howitt 2000).[1]

It is felt that a more balanced approach to understanding money and markets would consist of both theorizing and historical fact. After all, the main objective is to explain (understand) our current exchange technology (producer-merchant), not hypothetical exchange technologies. To this end, we now turn and examine the development of various exchange technologies throughout the ages.

Exchange Throughout the Ages

In this section, we examine briefly the evolution of specialization and exchange throughout the ages, beginning with the upper Paleolithic era. The underlying motive is relatively straightforward, namely, to search for clues about the underlying nature of large-scale specialization and exchange (Beaudreau 2005). To simplify the task, we use the exchange technology taxonomy summarized in Table 2.1. There are, in general, two types of exchange, non-intermediated and intermediated, the former consisting of what amounts to spontaneous exchange/trade among economic agents, and the latter, involving specialized agents.

Non-intermediated exchange can be further broken down into simple double-coincidence of wants barter, and monetary exchange (involving a numéraire-money). Intermediated exchange is broken down into merchant-intermediated (coordinated) exchange, and producer-merchant-intermediated exchange. Merchant-intermediated exchange, as the title implies, involves exchange in the presence of a merchant who oversees the purchase and sale of commodities. Producer-merchant-intermediated exchange involves the presence of producers and merchants (distinct individuals) who oversee the purchase of factor services in the case of the producer, and output in the case of the merchant.

Table 2.1
Exchange Technologies

Non–Intermediated	*Intermediated*
Double Coincidence of Wants	Merchant-Intermediated
Monetary Exchange	Producer-Merchant Intermediated

How did money as we know it today arise? In what conditions? Was large-scale specialization the result of money, or vice versa? Or, were these developments simultaneous? What was (were) the key factor(s)? Where and when? As it turns out, the existing literature on money and monetary theory provides little in the way of satisfactory answers to these questions. It does, however, address and answer questions such as whether a monetary equilibrium exists, and whether it was unique? Should money be included in the utility function? should money be included in the production function? Is money neutral—super neutral? What is the appropriate definition of money?

Consequently, our current understanding of the origins of money is limited, not to mention limiting, and can be summarized in terms of the following parable. Consider the case of two agents, each having endowments of goods, and each having preferences defined over these goods. Assuming that the endowment does not lie in the core, it follows that trade between these two agents will be Pareto improving. Each can be made better off by exchanging some of the abundant good against the scarce good. Next, introduce a third agent, and relax the double-coincidence of wants. In this case, single pair-wise exchanges are not Pareto improving. One party is made better of, while the other is made worse off. Introducing a numéraire solves the underlying problem. Next, introduce incomplete information. Suppose that agents have either no information or limited information on trading opportunities. Again, in this case, the introduction of a numéraire would be Pareto improving. Money decreases information costs, storage costs, transport costs, etcetera.

In short, money emerged spontaneously as a means to minimize the costs of exchange. By reducing information costs, transportation costs, and storage costs, it contributed to raising social welfare. This view is ubiquitous in the literature. Take, for example, Olivier Blanchard and Stanley Fischer's *Lectures on Macroeconomics*:

> Money plays two distinct roles in the economy: money is the medium of exchange, and it is usually also the unit of account. As a medium of exchange, it must be held between exchanges and thus also serves also a store of value. As a store of value, however, many other assets dominate it. The unit of account and medium of exchange functions of money are conceptually distinct and have sometimes been distinct in practice, especially during times of high inflation when a foreign money is, often used as unit of account while the local money continues to be used as medium of exchange. In this chapter we focus on money as a medium of exchange. Whether it is also the unit of account is of little relevance to the issues at hand. Later in the book, when we study business cycles, we will consider how both roles may combine to generate a potential role of money in business cycle fluctuations. Early monies took the form of commodities whose value in exchange was equal to their consumption value as commodities. The fact that these commodities were used as money raised their relative price. In contrast, the value of an unbacked, noncommodity money such as modern money derives only from the fact that it can be exchanged. (Blanchard and Fischer 1989, 154)

The historical and archeological literature on the origins of money, however, provides a widely contrasting account of the origins of money. Specifically, the historical and archeological records show that governments struck virtually all early monies, be they the pharaohs, kings, despots, or czars. According to Heather Pringle, money first appeared in ancient Mesopotamia.

> In all likelihood, human beings first being contemplating cash just about the time that Mesopotamians were slathering mortar on mud bricks to build the worlds first cities. To furnish these new temples and to serve temple officials, many farmers became artisans, stonemasons, silversmiths, tanners, weavers, boat builders, furniture makers. And within a few centuries, the cities became much greater than the sum of their parts. Economic life flourished and grew increasingly complex. Just how complex life grew in these early metropolises can be glimpsed in the world's oldest accounting records: 8,612 tiny clay tokens excavated from the floors of village houses and city temples across the Near East and studied in detail by Denise

Schmand-Besserat, an archeologist at the University of Texas at Austin. The tokens served first as counters, and perhaps later as promissory notes given to tax collectors before writing appeared. (Pringle 1998)

Moreover, there is no archeological evidence of the existence of non-government monies.[2] In other words, there is no evidence that monetary exchange emerged spontaneously in an n agent environment with transactions costs.

Based on the evidence found in the historical and archeological records, money, in its current form, was not a spontaneous development involving optimizing Nash (read: private) agents, but, rather, was a product of empire building (agglomeration), which, we define as the increasing size, expanse, and reach of civil administrations (centralization). Contrary to the current view, money and the current form of exchange organized around specialized traders (producers and merchants) evolved in response to government, specifically, to the problem of public choice-induced specialization, and the resulting coordinating and exchange problems. As we shall attempt to show, without large-scale government, the current exchange technology (money and specialized traders) may not have evolved.

MONEY: AN EMPIRICALLY-CONSISTENT ACCOUNT

A reading of both the recent literature on money and trade in the ancient economy, and the history of the ancient and modern economy revealed a number of what we shall, for want of a better word, refer to as "regularities." These include the fact that early monies are all, without exception, specific to large political—governmental—entities. By large, it should be understood, more important than the local tribe, or groupings of local tribes. All were struck by governments/rulers. And, all coexisted with taxation of one form or another. There is no evidence, at least to my knowledge, of private monies (i.e. non-governmental) in the ancient world—in spite of the presence of specialized traders.

How can these "regularities" be explained? Part of the answer, we believe, lies with developments in the art of governing, specifically, in the art of governing large geographical expanses (e.g. Sumeria, Mesopotamia, China, Persia, Rome, etcetera). By "governing," it should be understood "public choice."

On November 25, 1695, my paternal ancestor, Urbain Baudereau dit Graveline, an immigrant to Canada from France, was killed in a skirmish with Iroquois warriors intent on wiping out the colony on the island of Montreal—or, at the very least, weaken it. A crown prosecutor and colonist by day, he was a member of the colonial militia, ready to defend the then-young colony from attack. Contrast this with the Roman empire, and its 2,000,000 permanent troops, stationed throughout much of the Mediterranean basin, and beyond. Roman legionnaires were full-time soldiers, specialized in the art of war—or defense. Citizens of the Roman empire, regardless of their views on issues such as war and defense, consumed "military services," paid for out of government revenues, the most important source of which was taxes on its citizens.

These two cases represent opposites on the public goods spectrum. In the case of my ancestor, defense services (public good) were provided by all able-bodied citizens. There was no specialization, and hence, no need for trade. By contrast, Roman legionnaires were defense professionals (specialists) skilled in the art of war (defense). Clearly, while my ancestor could live off of the spoils of his land (autarky), Roman legionnaires depended on government (society) for their livelihood (specialization).

This brings us to the question of trade. How is trade for government services (defense, religion) in large geopolitical agglomerations carried out? How do these societies go about allocating a portion of what it produces to those who provide services to the state? Theoretically, there are a number of options. We shall focus on two, namely hierarchy and markets. we begin with hierarchy. In this case, the state, through its administrative officers, appropriates goods—and services—from its citizens in the form of a tax or levy. These are then used to remunerate the providers of public goods (armies, civil servants, government members). Provided that the government is organized efficiently (with a system of warehouses and bookkeeping), there is no reason to doubt the success of such a system.

By contrast, a society (via its government) could choose a system based on money and markets. In this case, the government issues money (bronze coins, for example), declares it legal tender, and requires that taxes be paid in it. To be more precise, the government issues coinage, uses it to purchase goods and services, and then imposes taxes and levies on its subjects, payable in its coinage (i.e. legal tender). In time, organized markets appear, complete with merchants who buy and sell goods.[3]

A system based on money, (royal) merchants and markets would have numerous advantages over one based on hierarchies (centralized). For one, governments would not have to devote scarce resources to the day-to-day operation of empire-wide exchange. More importantly, the decision of what to produce, and in what quantities, would be left to the merchant class. The problem of unused inventories would, as such, be eliminated. Another advantage is the possibility of extra-empire trade. For example, a government, by issuing new coins, could raise resources for a military strike in very little time. If its money was accepted outside of the empire, then it could benefit from increased seignorage.

History shows, quite decisively, that a system based on money, merchants and markets was preferred by most sovereigns to one based on hierarchies, and, a clear preference for sovereigns of large nation states and empires. In fact, one could go as far as to argue that money, merchants and markets were as important to the Sumerian, Persian, Chinese, Greek, and Roman empires as military acumen. It therefore follows that, notwithstanding isolated instances of money evolving spontaneously among optimizing agents (POW camps, etcetera), money as we know it today should be viewed as a creation of the state, specifically of public choice in large agglomerations. More important is the fact that money, merchants and markets were simultaneous developments, all having their origins—at least in their current form—in large political agglomerations.[4]

MONEY, MERCHANTS, TAXES AND "MAKING THE MARKET"

It is my view that an in-depth appreciation of the history of money, merchants, markets and taxes is an important input into understanding—and ultimately modelling—the process of exchange in modern societies. Take, for example, merchants. What do they do? How do they go about doing it? What are the associated risks? Historically, royal merchants were middlemen, intermediating between consumers (society, government) and producers, purchasing goods from the latter, and selling them to the former, using money as the means of payment. Chief among their concerns, however, were the problems of forecasting demand, and coordinating supply. If a Roman wheat merchant overestimated the demand for wheat, then he would find himself with unsold inventories. On the other hand, if he underestimated it, then he risked losing sales, and, more importantly, losing long-standing customers—perhaps even the local government.

Given the nature of early market exchange (i.e. involving government procurement), it stands to reason that government expenditure, defined generally, was the prime determinant of merchant activity. Put differently, governments, by way of their purchases, "made the market." For example, a planned military expedition in a foreign land would no doubt lead merchants to increase their orders for military boots, clothing, and armaments. The government would use its coinage to finance the purchase of goods and services. This money would then find its way into royal and private merchants' coffers, and ultimately, into the pockets of suppliers, who would have to remit a portion of it to the government in the form of taxes. The circle would be complete. The government would have received its goods and services, the people would have received government services, and, lastly, the government would have recuperated its coinage.

It bears noting that while merchants were ultimately responsible for creating income (i.e. from the purchase of goods and services), it was government expenditure that determined the level of market-based economic activity. We refer to this as "making the market." In general, merchants did not spontaneously increase orders of goods in anticipation of greater demand on the part of private citizens—although, theoretically, they could have. The risks of doing so were too great. What if the anticipated increase in demand did not materialize? Moreover, there were strategic problems. While increasing orders from producers would increase overall income, there was no guarantee that the demand for the individual merchant in question's wares would increase. Put differently, an individual merchant intent on increasing purchases of, say, boots, could not count on the producers of boots (the recipients of his income—trade credit) to purchase his output (i.e. the boots). As we will go on to argue, the problem of income creation (i.e. making the market) is strategic in nature, owing in large measure to the public or social nature of monetary income. If a single merchant increases orders from suppliers, then there is little chance it will succeed in selling its merchandize, for lack of buyers. However, if all merchants do so, then overall income will increase, thus increasing the chances of selling the goods in question.

This, we argue, explains the paucity of spontaneous trade in pre-industrial economies (i.e. before the 19th century). Rather, exchange in pre-industrial economies was limited, for the most part, to what we refer to as public goods, specifically government and religious services (Findlay 1973; Garnsey, Hopkins and Whittaker 1983), giving rise to "public good-based trade."

THE EMERGENCE OF SPONTANEOUS TRADE

It is fair to say that the history of trade as defined here is, for all intents and purposes, dominated by public goods and government, spontaneous trade being a relatively new phenomenon.[5] Public choice-related trade, by which it should be understood, trade involving government/religious services, is, like civilization itself, over five thousand years old.[6] The emergence of spontaneous trade, on the other hand, is a relatively recent phenomenon. This raises a number of questions, including when, why and how did spontaneous trade emerge?[7]

Spontaneous trade, we argue, was the result of a number of factors. First, there was the growing disenchantment in the 18th century with imperial governments, and, consequently, with mercantilism. Government hierarchies had grown considerably, as had their costs (government revenue). The Physiocratic movement in France, headed by Anne-Robert Jacques Turgot and Francois Quesnay, and the American Revolution bear testimony to the growing disenchantment with government as the ultimate arbitrator of wealth. Second, there were technology shocks. Richard Arkwright's spinning jenny, James Watt's high-efficiency steam engine and reciprocating engine (with James Boulton) set the stage for a new form of wealth creation, namely inanimate energy-based manufacturing. These two factors, we argue, contributed to a paradigm shift in Western civilization. Wealth appropriation through trade (mercantilism) was replaced by wealth creation through manufacture (processing, adding value, value added, industry).[8]

The distinguishing feature in so far as high-throughput manufacturing is concerned was its spontaneous nature—that is, independent of government. While some former royal merchants invested in manufacturing, most industrialists were non-governmental. The important point, as far as exchange technology is concerned, is that trade would never be the same. From this point on, private merchants and private producers would have to, collectively, "make the market."

Governments could no longer be counted on to "make the market." As we shall argue throughout this book, while the history of inanimate energy-based civilization is glorious, the story of producer-merchant mediated exchange is punctuated by episodes of despair and depression, based, in large measure, on the nature of the underlying Schelling-type coordination game, more specifically, on the inability of private merchants and producers to "make markets" commensurately with their ability to create wealth, which, as we have argued elsewhere, is intimately tied to its use of inanimate energy (Beaudreau 1996,1998,1999). In the next section, we present a simple model that captures the essence of producer-merchant exchange.

A Model of Producer-Merchant Exchange

Despite a long illustrious history, merchant exchange and producer-merchant exchange have been absent and continue to be absent from mainstream economics. In microeconomics, there is no mention whatsoever of the merchant's problem (Henderson and Quandt 1980; Varian 1992). That is, buying with the intent of reselling.[9] For roughly a century, trade has been modelled as a spontaneous activity that takes place in fictitious markets (Walrasian), guided by Adam Smith's invisible hand .

There have been exceptions, including Knut Wicksell's description of exchange in his 1898 *Interest and Prices*, Clifford H. (Major) Douglas' description of exchange in an industrial economy, and Frederich Hayek's description of exchange in his work on inflation. More recent examples of non-Walrasian-based exchange include Benjamin Bental and Benjamin Eden's work on uncertain and sequential trade (UST) economies (Bental and Eden, 1996).

While an improvement over Walrasian models, these models fail to capture the essence of uncertain and sequential trade, namely the presence of specialized traders (coordinating agents). As my brief history of exchange has shown, merchants have, from the beginning, played an integral part in exchange—to the point of defining it. This section presents a simple model of producer-merchant exchange, which mimics the exchange process in modern industrialized economies.

BANKERS AND BANKING

To begin with, we assume the existence of a single merchant banker, who, by government decree (fiat), has the right to extend credit to producers and merchants.[10] Credit notes and bills of exchange are the relevant credit instruments. For our purposes, we will assume that credit is a free good. That is, there are no costs to producers and merchants associated with using credit to finance their activities. As such, the value of the banker's assets must be identically equal to the value of his liabilities.

PRODUCERS AND MERCHANTS

We consider an environment in which there exist $2n$ producers and one merchant, the former transforming raw materials using capital and labor into consumption and capital goods, and the latter buying and selling these goods (transformation) at a fixed point in geographical space (shop).[11] As such, value added is assumed to be an increasing function of capital and labor.[12]

Variables

V_{ic} = consumption good producer i's value added.
V_{ik} = capital good producer i's value added.
ω_{ic} = consumption good producer i's demand for working capital.
ω_{ik} = capital good producer i's demand for working capital.
π_{ic} = consumption good producer i's profits.
π_{ik} = capital good producer i's profits.
V_c = aggregate consumption good value added.
V_k = aggregate capital good value added.
ω_c = aggregate consumption good producers' demand for working capital.
ω_k = aggregate capital good producers' demand for working capital.
ω_m = merchant demand for working capital.
π_c = aggregate consumption good producer profits.
π_k = aggregate capital good producer profits.
α = working capital's average and marginal value product.
β = consumption good overall income elasticity.

Equations

$$V_{ic} = \alpha\omega_{ic} \tag{2.1}$$

$$V_{ik} = \alpha\omega_i \tag{2.2}$$

$$V_c = \alpha\omega_c \tag{2.3}$$

$$V_k = \alpha\omega_k \tag{2.4}$$

$$V_c = \sum_{i=1}^{n} V_{ic} \tag{2.5}$$

$$V_k = \sum_{i=1}^{n} V_{ik} \tag{2.6}$$

$$\omega_c = \sum_{i=1}^{n} \omega_{ic} \qquad (2.7)$$

$$\omega_k = \sum_{i=1}^{n} \omega_{ik} \qquad (2.8)$$

$$\omega_m = V_c + V_k \qquad (2.9)$$

$$\pi_{ic} = 1/n \left[\beta\omega_m \right] - \omega_i \qquad (2.10)$$

$$\pi_{ik} = 1/n \left[(1 - \beta)\omega_m \right] - \omega_{ik} \qquad (2.11)$$

$$\pi_c = \sum_{i=1}^{n} \pi_{ic} \qquad (2.12)$$

$$\pi_k = \sum_{i=1}^{n} \pi_{ik} \qquad (2.13)$$

THE EXCHANGE AND PRODUCTION PROCESSES

As pointed out, exchange and production in this model is sequential in nature. Specifically, to begin with, consumption and capital good producers acquire working capital (at the bank) with which to hire the variable factor inputs, in this case, labor. The actual production functions are defined in Equations 2.1 and 2.2. Value added in both sectors is increasing in the level of working capital.[13] Working capital, in this case, is a proxy for all variable factor inputs. The aggregate levels of working capital and value added are determined by Equations 2.5 to 2.8. It is important to point out that the demand for working capital on the part of producers is less than the level of value added by an amount equal to profits. Profits, in this case, are a residual form of payment, made once output has been sold to the merchant.[14] The demand for working capital on the latter's behalf (Equation 2.9) is assumed, to begin with, to be equal to aggregate value added, defined as the sum of V_c and V_k. Producer profits (consumption and capital good firms) are defined by Equations 2.10 and 2.11. We see that the representative consumption good producer's profits are, by definition, equal to its share of the merchant's working capital allocated to consumption goods, defined here as $\beta\omega_m$, where β is its share [$0<\beta<1$] minus its own demand for working capital, ω_{ic}. Equation 2.13 describes capital good producer's profits.

To simplify matters, it is assumed that the demand for consumption goods is equal to the aggregate wage bill ($\beta\omega_m = \omega_c + \omega_k$), and that the demand for capital goods is equal to aggregate profits (($1-\beta\omega_m$)($\pi_c + \pi_k$)). These are simplifying assumptions which have no bearing whatsoever on the results. Once product markets have cleared, merchants use the proceeds to pay off the loans (working capital) they took out to finance trade. It is assumed that merchants have no costs, and, hence, earn no income (i.e. percentage of sales).[15]

Equilibrium Conditions

Equilibrium, as far as the present model is concerned, will be defined in terms of value added, working capital, and profits. Equations 2.14–2.16 define equilibrium in the consumption good, capital good, and merchant sectors of the economy. In the case of consumption good sector, equilibrium requires that the value of output be equal to the aggregate level of consumption and capital good producer working capital, firm working capital being the key variable in the demand for consumption goods. In the case of the capital goods sector, equilibrium requires that the value of output be equal to the aggregate level of consumption and capital good producer profits. Lastly, in the case of the merchant, equilibrium requires that its overall level of working capital be equal to aggregate value added (consumption and capital goods), which, via Equation 2.16, is equal to the aggregate wage bill and aggregate profits.

$$V_c = \omega_c + \omega_k \tag{2.14}$$

$$V_k = \pi_c + \pi_k \tag{2.15}$$

$$\omega_m = V_c + V_k = \omega_c + \omega_k + \pi_c + \pi_k \tag{2.16}$$

THE DEMAND FOR MONEY

The demand for money in a producer-merchant model of an exchange economy differs from conventional models in a number of important ways (Laidler 1977, 1990). First, two sets of agents demand money (working capital, credit), namely producers who coordinate production, and the merchant (merchants) who coordinates distribution. Producers demand working capital (money) in order to transact in factor markets (i.e. acquire variable inputs). Formally, this is captured by Equations 2.17-2.18 which are obtained by inverting Equations 2.1 and 2.2. As such, $(1/\alpha)$ should as such be seen as the demand for credit per dollar of value added. For example, if α takes on the value of 1.4285, then the value-added elasticity of the demand for credit is 0.70. As for the merchant, s/he demands working capital to finance the purchase of goods (rolling stock). This is captured by Equation 2.19 above.

$$\omega_{ic} = (1/\alpha)V_{ic} \tag{2.17}$$

$$\omega_{ik} = (1/\alpha)V_{ik} \tag{2.18}$$

From this, it follows that the elasticity of the overall demand for money per unit of value added exceeds unity. That is, for V_{ic} of value added (consumption and capital good), the demand for money is $\omega_{ic} + V_{ic}$ This reflects the fact that value added undergoes two transformations, namely its initial transformation (producer) and its secondary transformation (merchant). It should be pointed out, however, that, at any one point in time, the demand for credit can never be greater than the amount of the value added.

Relationship to the Demand for Money Literature

This view of the demand for money differs in many ways from the standard view found in the literature (Laidler 1977,1993). In conventional models, the demand for money on the part of agents is an increasing function of income, and a decreasing function of the opportunity cost of holding cash balances. Here, it is modelled as an increasing function of consumption and capital goods firms' and the merchant's demand for working capital. This, we maintain, captures more accurately the integral role of producers and merchants in the demand for money.

It should, however, be pointed out that while it is somewhat orthogonal to the existing literature, it does, nonetheless, address a number of criticisms levelled, over the course of the past century, at work on the demand for money literature. Consider, for example, Harold Moulton's remarks regarding "Money in Relation to Production."

> When money is spoken of as a medium of exchange, one usually has in mind the exchange of consumer goods. For convenience of exposition, eco-

nomic treatises have commonly been divided into four parts, devoted respectively to consumption, production, exchange, and distribution. Money is treated under exchange and its chief function is usually regarded as that of affecting the exchange of goods that have already been produced and are in the market awaiting transfer to the hands of those who are to consume them. But if one is to appreciate fully the significance of money under a capitalistic industrial regime, it is necessary to consider the part that it plays in the productive as well as in the exchange process. Exchange of consumers' goods is not to be excluded; but the role of money in getting goods ready to be exchanged as completed products must be included. Modern business is almost universally conducted through the use of money. With money the manufacturer purchases the materials needed for the construction of his plant; with money he employs an administrative staff to manage his business; and with money he purchases the raw materials and supplies and employs the labor force required to operate his business. In a similar way producers of raw materials, transportation agencies, and wholesalers and retailers employ money in connection with every other phase of their business operations; under modern conditions even the farmer makes an extensive use of money. In short, practically the entire production process is nowadays organized and operated through the use of money.... Because of the great importance that has always been attached to money as capital, the economist has been wise in laying emphasis upon the fact that real capital consists of tangible properties. However, this emphasis has in turn tended to minimize the significant part that money plays in a capitalistic society. Productive instruments cannot be made effective in the service of society unless liquid capital is available with which to assemble raw materials and labor power in producing organizations. (Moulton 1938, 21)

A similar critique is found in Williford I. King's 1920 *American Economic Review* article entitled "Circulating Capital: Its Nature and Relation to the Public Welfare:"

Despite the fact that bank notes or deposits are used in the daily business of hundreds of millions of people, there still remain numerous misconceptions concerning the nature of these media of exchange. Furthermore, it seems safe to assert that few indeed, not only the users but also of the bankers who issue the obligations, have any clear idea of just what effects upon the public such issues produce. According to the writers observation, textbooks in economics rarely touch upon this last and most important phase of the problem. It therefore appears to be worthwhile to discuss in some detail the fundamental principles connected with bank credit. Bank credit is used mainly for business purposes. Some loans from banks are obtained in order to purchase consumption goods, but loans for this purpose form so small a fraction of the total that they scarcely need consideration here. The bulk of credit loaned, not only by banks, but by other lenders as well, is nowadays borrowed for purposes of investment or the use in the undertakings for profit making. (King 1920, 738)

The producer-merchant model of exchange, we submit, addresses these concerns, and, moreover, provides an empirically-consistent model of the exchange process in industrial economies. Whereas in traditional analysis, the demand for money is modelled as an increasing function of aggregate income, here it is modelled as the outcome of optimizing individual producers and merchants.

MAKING GOODS AND MAKING MARKETS

This simple model of exchange makes a key, fundamental, and, until now, overlooked point about producers, namely that in addition to making goods and services, producers "make markets" via their transactions in factor markets. By increasing their demand for labor, they increase overall income, thus contributing to the activity that we refer to as "making of the market" (aggregate income). The corollary, it therefore follows, is what we refer to as "unmaking the market," which consists of reducing the demand for labor, and, as such, reducing overall income. These two aspects of producer behavior, unfortunately, are often ignored. Another overlooked aspect is the orthogonal nature of producers' factor market behavior and their product market behavior. Put differently, the income producers' generate (via ω_{ic}) will, in most cases, have little-to-no bearing on their sales, and hence revenue. In the model, a one dollar increase in operating capital will increase the representative consumption good producer's sales by $1/n$ dollar. As n increases, this share decreases, going to zero in the limit.

Perhaps this explains why it is common practice today to view the market (aggregate income-working capital) as being independent of producer costs. As such, decisions that affect the cost side of the ledger (working capital) are rarely seen as having an impact on the revenue side of the ledger. However, while this may hold true at the individual producer level, it does not hold true at the aggregate level, where aggregate producer behavior affects aggregate income, which affects aggregate merchant behavior, and so on and so forth.

SEQUENTIAL EXCHANGE, UNCERTAINTY AND EXPECTATIONS

Given the sequential nature of trade, it stands to reason that consumption and capital goods producers' decisions in factor markets will be predicated on their expectations regarding the overall economic activity, and, more specifically, the demand for their product(s). An anticipated increase in overall economic activity will increase producer demand for operating capital, and, hence, for value added. Similarly, the merchants' decisions in product markets (consumption and capital goods) will be predicated on their expectations regarding producer behavior as well as on aggregate merchant behavior.

This highlights the strategic nature of what could be referred to as the "making the market" game. Producers base their decisions on their expectations of what their fellow producers and merchants will do. The result is a class of expectational Nash equilibria.

Expectations

Let:

$[\omega_m]^e_{ic}$ = consumption good producer i's expectation of the overall level of merchant income.

$[\omega_m]^e_{ik}$ = capital good producer i's expectation of the overall level of merchant income.

V^e_c = the merchant's expectation of the overall level of consumption good output.

V^e_k = the merchant's expectation of the overall level of capital good output.

As one can clearly see, the problem of expectations is multi-dimensional. In the model, all $2n$ producers and the merchant are assumed to form their own expectations, which may or may not be identical. Just how they go about forming expectations, however, is beyond the scope of the present work. Suffice it to say that there are as many "expectational" equilibria as there are combinations of expectations.

To understand the role of expectations in the model, we examine various expectational equilibria. To this end, we assume that producers' and merchants' expectations are either (1) bullish, (2) bearish, or (3) status quo. This gives rise to a total of nine possible states of nature. These are shown in Table 2.2, along with the resulting macroeconomic outcomes.

As Table 2.2 shows, the model generates a number of expectational Nash equilibrium (Farmer 1996). These are sometimes referred to as "self-fulfilling prophecies." Consider the following example. Starting from an initial equilibrium, suppose that, for some reason, producers suddenly become bearish over the future, specifically, over the level of aggregate demand (i.e. ω).[16] Acting on these expectations, they then procede to decrease their demand for labor, and, consequently, the demand and supply of working capital. Merchants respond by decreasing planned orders of consumption and capital goods. As this case illustrates, expectations are self-fulfilling: the prophecy of lower sales "self-fulfills" itself. Producers expect lower sales, act accordingly, and, in the end, see their expectations fulfilled. The reverse situation also holds. In this case, bullish producers increase the overall demand for working capital, labor and capital. Merchants respond by increasing orders for consumption and capital goods, resulting in an increase in the level of overall output.

Table 2.2
Expectational Equilibria

P\M	Bearish	Status Quo	Bullish
Bearish	*Fall in Output*	*Excess Demand (P)*	*Excess Demand (P)*
Status Quo	*Excess Supply (P)*	*Status Quo*	*Excess Demand (M)*
Bullish	*Excess Supply (P)*	*Excess Supply (P)*	*Increase in Output*

As these examples clearly illustrate, a necessary condition for an expectational equilibrium to exist is the presence of "passive" merchants. Specifically, in both of these cases, merchants simply validated producers' expectations, decreasing orders in bearish markets, and increasing orders in bullish markets. Consider the case, however, where merchant expectations are independent of producers' expectations. Could expectations be self-fulfilling as was the case above? As it turns out, there are a number of possibilities, illustrated in Table 2.2. If producers and merchants are bearish, then the outcome will be bearish, for obvious reasons. If producers are bearish, but merchants are neutral (*status quo*) (order last period's quantities), then there is a good chance that the outcome will be the status quo. The reason is straightforward, namely that merchants' orders do not decrease, prompting producers to revise their expectations upwards. If producers are bullish, and merchants are bearish, then there is a good chance that overall output and income will increase. In this case, producers', by increasing the demand for factor inputs, increase overall factor income, prompting merchants to revise their expectations upwards, thus leading, at least conceivable, to an increase in overall output and income.[17]

Inventories

This raises a number of questions. For example, how are these equilibria affected by the presence of inventories? Thus far, we have ignored inventories. We know, however, that both merchants and producers carry (hold) them. As it turns out, inventories have a stabilizing effect on the level of aggregate economic activity. To see this, consider the off-diagonal terms in Table 2.2. In the case in which producers are bearish and merchants are bullish, an excess demand for consumer and capital goods results as merchants increase their supplies. If producers do not hold inventories, then there arises the possibility that merchants may turn bearish on the future, and, seeing that producers are actually decreasing their output, revise their orders. The presence of inventories, however, allows merchants to realize their objectives. Thus, in lieu of signaling their desire for more consumption and capital goods via back orders, they do so via sales.

There is also the question of intra-cohort expectations. If individual consumption good producers hold inventories, then they can hedge against a bad outcome. For example, if merchants are bullish and other producers are bullish, then a bearish consumption good producer, by holding inventories, can minimize the costs of erring (expectation-wise), so to speak.

A Model of Producer-Merchant Exchange with Technology Shocks

This simple framework provides an empirically-consistent model of exchange in an advanced industrial setting. It highlights the important role played by merchants, both individually and collectively, in determining the overall level of output, employment and income. Until now, merchants have been absent from macroeconomic—and microeconomic—models. In this section, we examine the properties of the resulting equilibria, specifically with regard to perturbations (shocks).

Suppose that the hypothetical economy described above is hit by an output-increasing Hicks-neutral technology shock. That is, existing labor and capital are now τ percent more productive. The relevant question is whether it can successfully make the transition to a higher equilibrium growth path in response to such a shock?[18] If so, how? If not, why not? We show that owing to the nature of the game played by profit-maximizing producers, and the fact that profits are a residual form of income, a producer-merchant exchange-based economy cannot make a nominal transition to the higher equilibrium growth path. We refer to the resulting equilibrium as one of income inertia, or, quite simply, underincome. Individual firms have no private incentives to increase wages, and hence, working capital. In light of this, merchants have no private incentives to increase orders of consumption and capital goods. Paradoxically, the economy suffers from inertia, in spite of improved fundamentals.

PRIVATE INCENTIVES

To demonstrate this, consider Equations 2.10 and 2.11 which describe the individual producer's optimization problem. In a Nash setting (*ceteris paribus*), increasing one's wage τ percent—in keeping with labor productivity—will increase the firm's overall costs by more than it will increase its revenue. This is shown via Equations 2.19–2.20, where for all values of β/n less than 1, $d\pi_{ic}$ is less than zero.

Proposition 1: In the Schelling-type wage-setting producer-merchant environment described here, there are no private incentives for producers to increase working capital (income) in response to a capacity-increasing technology shock.

Proposition 2: In the Schelling-type wage-setting producer-merchant environment described here, overall working capital (income) fails to rise commensurately with a generalized capacity-increasing technology shock.

Proof:

These can be reduced to:

$$d\pi_{ic} = 1/n \, [\beta d\omega_{ic}] - d\omega_{ic} \qquad (2.19)$$

$$d\pi_{ik} = 1/n \, [(1-\beta)d\omega_{ik}] - d\omega_{ic} \qquad (2.20)$$

For all values of β/n less than 1, $d\pi_{ic}$ and $d\pi_{ik}$ are less than zero. As 2.19 and 2.20 hold for all producers, it follows that private producers have no incentive to increase working capital, which, implies that, in the aggregate, economy-wide working capital will fail to increase commensurately with overall productive capacity. *QED*

In other words, *ceteris paribus*, increasing working capital—wages—decreases producer profits. The optimal response, as far as the individual producer is concerned, is to not increase one's wage. The resulting Nash equilibrium, it therefore follows, is characterized by what we refer to as income inertia.[19] Income inertia can also be viewed as an income and output indeterminacy. Given the nature of the Schelling-type coordination game (Nash), there are no private incentives to act, resulting in collective inertia.

This raises a number of counterfactual questions. For example, could expectations overcome the inertia (underincome)? Could bullish merchants, by increasing orders of consumption and capital goods, push the economy on to the higher growth path? Theoretically, if a hypothetical bullish merchant increased orders by τ percent, then, in the short-run at least, the economy would operate at capacity. Producers would increase shipments to the merchant by τ percent. Assuming that wage rates remain constant, consumption and capital goods firms would earn windfall profits.[20] Unfortunately, this would not be sustainable in the long run as a glut of consumption—and ultimately capital—goods would appear. The τ percent more consumption goods would go unsold, which, in the medium-to-long term would lead producers to decrease their demand for capital goods, thus aborting eventually a merchant-led transition.

RATIONALIZATION

Thus far, we have established that there are no private incentives for producers to increase their demand for working capital (wages) in response to the technology shock. The next question is whether this is the best they can do? For example, could they do better by reducing their demand for working capital? Remember, production processes are now τ percent more productive.

As it turns out, it can easily be shown that by reducing working capital by τ percent, profits will increase. The reason has to do with the fact that each productive factor is now τ percent more productive. Producers can now fill their orders (from merchants) with τ percent fewer factor inputs. We refer to such a strategy as rationalization. We argue that, in general, rationalization and underincome go hand-in-hand, with causality running from the latter to the former. Paradoxically, higher productivity leads to lower employment.

Theoretically, at least, rationalization, at the aggregate level, can lead the producer-merchant economy described here into a downward spiral, for obvious reasons. If all producers cut working capital (employment) by τ percent, then ω_c and ω_k will fall by τ percent, thus leading merchants to decrease their orders for consumption and capital goods by τ percent, setting off a second round of layoffs. Where the ensuing downward spiral ends will depend on the underlying production technology. If there are technological limits to cutting employment (fixed labor input), then it follows that only when these limits are reached will the spiral end. If the technology is strictly linear, however, the equilibrium will be the null set.

Real Transitions

The model developed in this chapter assumes fixed prices (wages and product prices). Quantities both of consumption and capital goods, and labor—not to mention energy and intermediate inputs—increase and/or decrease, with prices remaining constant. It therefore follows that the problem of underincome as modelled here is essentially a nominal phenomenon—that is, one in which product prices, specifically product-price adjustment, have no role to play. As prices are variable, the question of product-price adjustment arises. For example, could product-price adjustment (downward) increase real income, and in the process, pave the way for a real transition to the growth path? Specifically, decreasing product prices, by increasing real wages (operating income divided by prices), increase the demand for consumption and capital goods, prompting merchants to increase orders from producers, thus resulting in a successful transition. In this case, while nominal income, measured by aggregate working capital, would remain constant, real income would increase by τ percent.

Among the key issues, as far as real transitions are concerned, is the question of downward price adjustment in the presence of technological change—specifically, will producers, finding themselves with τ percent more capacity, decrease product price by an equivalent amount, assuming of course that the τ is a free-good?[21] The answer is by no means obvious. First, if producer ic decreases his/her price by τ percent, then s/he runs the risk of incurring loses should demand does not increase by at least τ percent. In other words, without a guarantee that demand will increase by, at the very least, τ percent, producer ic will choose not to decrease price. However, if s/he goes ahead and does reduce price, then pressure will mount to decrease operating costs, specifically labor costs, prompting calls for wage decreases.

Another important issue is the producer-merchant relationship. Specifically, will the merchant agree to reduce the sticker price of producer i's good, in the presence of markup pricing. That is, if the merchant operates on a mark-up basis, s/he may be reluctant to decrease price, as it would decrease his/her revenues. Another merchant-related issue is the question of shelf space. Will the merchant increase producer i's shelf space at the expense of competitors? This raises the strategic aspects of price decreases. How will competitors react? Will they stand pat, and watch their market share diminish? Will they react? Will possible reprisals act as a deterrent?

This raises the possibility of price-related coordination failures. In producer i's eyes, a price decrease—by τ percent—will be tolerated so long as all other producers (consumption and capital good) decrease their prices by an equivalent amount. Real profits will increase by τ percent. On the other hand, if s/he is the only one to act (i.e. decrease price), then there may be some reluctance. First, there is the question of own-price elasticity. Will demand increase sufficiently to increase profits? Will merchants stock more of his/her product at the expense of rivals? Will rivals stand pat? If all producers cut prices, will they be better off? Clearly, in a world of incomplete information, coordination failures are not only possible, but highly probable. Individually, producers will be reluctant to decrease prices, not knowing what his/her rivals will do, let alone all other $2n$-1 producers.

WHO MAKES THE MARKET?

As we have shown, the presence of productive capacity is not a sufficient condition for wealth, as classical and neoclassical writers believed. Say's Law, as such, is valid in equilibrium, but not out of equilibrium. Nominal and real coordination failures, as has been shown here, preclude transitions to higher equilibrium growth paths in response to technological change.

This raises the ultimate question, as far as dynamic macroeconomics is concerned, namely in periods of technological change, who "makes the market?" Who increases nominal/real income commensurately with productive capacity? Is it individual producers who, in Smithian fashion, by looking out for their own good, contribute to the good of society? The results presented above suggest that owing to the nature of the game (wage and price) played by producers, private Nash economies cannot make the transition to new equilibrium growth paths. Individual producers have no private incentives to increase nominal income. Increasing nominal income in line with productivity, *ceteris paribus*, is a profit-decreasing strategy. Decreasing product price, as pointed out above, can also be a profit-decreasing strategy.

In short, while producers make the market in equilibrium, no one (merchant or producer) stands prepared to make the market out of equilibrium. The result is a classical prisoner's dilemma, where cooperative strategies are dominated by non-cooperative ones, where cooperative behavior is dominated by non-cooperative behavior.

The result is a class of paradoxical equilibria. For example, income, supply and demand could be nil in spite of positive, system-wide capacity, for lack of a merchant, for lack of income, or for lack of optimistic expectations. Technological change, it therefore follows, need not necessarily result in increased wealth and prosperity, as pointed out by Sturgeon Bell.

Policy Measures

Profit-maximizing producers have no private interest to increase wages (working capital) in response to a Hicks-neutral technology shock. Likewise, profit-maximizing merchants have no private interest to increase orders of consumption and capital goods, given the absence of higher wages (aggregate working capital). The result is underincome and inertia. The relevant question then is, can anything be done? Can the inertia be reversed? If so, how? Here, we examine briefly some of the measures which could, at least theoretically, solve the problem of underincome. These include (1) commercial policy (2) government expenditure (3) government-based wage and price setting.

Before examining these, it is important to highlight the public-good aspects of markets, as defined in this chapter. From the producer's point of view, the market is a public good. When a producer hires a worker, s/he creates income (working capital) which benefits all producers and merchants. There is, for lack of a better word, a "market externality." Producers that reduce working capital can, as such, be viewed as free-riders in the public-good sense of the term. That is, they free-ride off of the "markets" made by others.

COMMERICAL POLICY

Underincome, as argued earlier, results from the presence of income inertia on the part of producers. At the individual producer level, potential wealth (value added) increases; however producer working capital does not. As aggregate producer working capital (ω_m) can, by definition, be no greater than the sum of individual producer working capital, inertia characterizes the economy as a whole. In other words, aggregate producer capital does not increase. This begs the question what policy measures, if any, can be taken to resolve this coordination failure, this case of income inertia?

One conceivable way to solve the problem without increasing national producer working capital (ω_c, ω_k) is to turn to foreign markets. Foreign markets (nominal income), created in large measure by the factor market decisions made by foreign producers, offer the possibility of increased sales and, consequently, increased profits to domestic producers. Liberalizing trade, it therefore follows, could, at least conceivably, provide domestic producers with the specter of higher sales and higher profits.

The downside, however, is the reciprocal nature of trade liberalization. Typically, access to foreign markets is obtained in return for access to domestic markets. Foreign merchant orders from domestic producers will, as a result, increase as will domestic merchants orders from foreign producers. Free trade, it therefore follows, can only be beneficial if the resulting exports exceed imports.[22]

In this case, the domestic country would either begin running a current account surplus, or increase an existing surplus. To this end, either domestic or foreign merchants would have to extend credit to foreign buyers. That is, domestic firms would have to accept foreign credit-based assets in return for their goods.[23] At the aggregate level, the country would run a current-account surplus and a capital-account deficit (in equilibrium).

Conceptually at least, commercial policy is analogous to third-party intervention. The *2n* Nash wage and price-setting firms that comprise the economy cannot, when behaving optimally, move the new growth path. A third party is needed, which, in this case, is the foreign merchant, trading goods against foreign liabilities.

Yet another response to the problem of underincome involving commercial policy is what we shall refer to as short-sighted import substitution, whereby the country in question raises tariffs on imported goods that compete directly with those sectors or industries experiencing the greatest excess capacity—that is, those that suffer the most from underincome. The idea here is to divert merchant orders away from imported products over to domestic products, and, in the process, increase domestic firm operating rates, revenue, profits and earning.

Clearly, this policy measure is short sighted, and ultimately destined to meet with failure. For one, it assumes that foreign income will not be affected (Nash assumption), and, secondly, that foreign governments will stand pat.

As we shall show, the Fordney-McCumber and Smoot-Hawley Tariff Acts are examples of commercial policy-based policy measures aimed at solving the problem of underincome, a problem their sponsors (especially Senator Reed Smoot) only partially understood.

GOVERNMENT EXPENDITURE

For traditionally-defined government expenditure to resolve the problem of income-inertia (underincome), the government must do more than tax, borrow and spend, for obvious reasons. Taxing, borrowing and spending does not increase the overall level of income; instead, it merely redistributes it. As such, traditional Keynesian-style macroeconomic policies are ineffective. For government expenditure to be successful, the government, like the merchant, must increase the overall level of working capital (ω_m); otherwise, the problem will remain whole.

The key, it therefore follows, lies in increasing the overall level of money income. As the government cannot set wages and prices, it stands to reason that it has no choice but to increase its liabilities. Consider the following example. Suppose that the consumption good/capital good split is 70-30. That is, 70 percent of national income is in the form of consumption goods, while 30 percent is in the form of capital goods. Also suppose that national income is $100.00, and that τ assumes a value of 0.05.

In this case, the government would borrow $3.50 from the private banking system with the intention of purchasing an equivalent amount of consumption goods. The merchant would then increase orders for consumption and capital goods by 5 percent. The government would then purchase $3.50 worth of consumption goods. As a result, consumption goods producers would see their profits rise by an equivalent amount. The government would then tax 70 percent of $3.50 ($2.45), leaving $1.05 in the form of increased profits. The latter would then be reinvested in capital equipment (purchased at the merchant).

In turn, capital goods firms' revenues and profits would rise by an equivalent amount. Overall sales would rise by $1.50, of which 70 percent would be taxed away, leaving $0.45 in profits for capital goods firms. Together with the proceeds from the taxation of consumption goods firms ($2.45), total tax receipts would be $3.50, the amount of the original loan (government liability). What is important to remember in this case is the recurrent nature of government intervention. Year in and year out, government would be called upon to purchase \$3.50 worth of consumption goods. The associated government debt—with private banks—would never be retired. In essence, these two cases represent a return of sorts to pre-industrial trade where, as pointed out earlier in this chapter, the government "made the market."

WAGE AND PRICE POLICY

A fully-informed government, fully aware of the problem of underincome and the subtleties of the prisoner's dilemma (*Propositions 1* and *2*), could, by setting wages and prices, orchestrate a successful transition to the new, higher equilibrium growth path. This would be achieved either by wage policy, price policy, or some combination thereof. In the above example, a government, by legislating a τ percent, across-the-board increase in wages (operating capital), in combination with a price freeze, could solve the underlying prisoner's dilemma. As such, V_c and V_k would increase by τ percent, increasing the demand for merchant credit by an equivalent amount, etcetera. These increases would then work their way through the economy, resulting in an across-the-board increase in economic magnitudes of τ percent, ensuring a successful transition to the new, higher equilibrium growth path.

Conversely, it could opt for a real transition. For example, it could legislate a τ percent across-the-board decrease in product prices in combination with a wage freeze. In this case, real wages would increase by τ percent, thus prompting the merchant to increase orders for consumption and capital goods by τ percent. As a result, real wages and real profits would increase by τ percent, as would the overall level of economic activity, thus ensuring a successful transition to the new growth path. Finally, it could choose to combine nominal wage increases with price decreases. In this case, the sum of wage increase, measured in percent, and the negative of the price decrease, also measured in percentage, ought to be equal to τ.

Summary

This chapter presented a formal model of producer-merchant exchange. Existing models of exchange were rejected in favor of a simple producer-merchant model that mimics the exchange technology found in western industrialized democracies. Underincome (income inertia) was derived as an equilibrium to the relevant Schelling-type coordination game. The sub-optimality of the resulting equilibrium led to a discussion of policy measures, including commercial policy and government expenditure. These results will now be used to examine two types of underincome, namely, energy deepening-based underincome, and nonenergy deepening-based underincome. The former refers to underincome that results from energy deepening, defined as an increase in the consumption of energy per period of time. The latter refers to underincome that results from organization-related technology shocks. Included among these is the recent trend towards workerless factories, where animate human supervision is replaced by inanimate computer-based supervision.

Appendix I: The Spontaneous Private Market Impossibility Theorem

In this chapter, it has been shown that, owing to the absence of private incentives to increase working capital (ω) in response to an economy-wide capacity-increasing technology shock, a private Nash producer-merchant economy cannot make the transition to the new higher equilibrium growth path corresponding to this technological shock. Put differently, starting from a point along a given aggregate value added growth path, private Nash economies cannot move to higher growth paths in response to a technology shock.

In this appendix, we generalize this result to all forms of intermediated exchange. Intermediated exchange differs from nonintermediated exchange by the presence of specialized traders in the former, and their absence in the latter. Nonintermediated exchange refers to exchange technologies without traders (specialized agents). Barter and primitive monetary exchange are examples. In the latter, an exchange medium (e.g. gold, silver, salt) exists, and is used in trade (see Table 2.1). Here, we show that intermediated forms of exchange cannot be supported as Nash equilibria, and hence, are unlikely to arise spontaneously. This has important implications for the history of monetary exchange. Specifically, it casts considerable doubt on the possibility of spontaneous emergence of markets and money.

Consider the simplest case of n producers (agents), each producing one unit of a differentiated good. Also assume, following Clower and Howitt (2000) that barter is too costly, and hence, not considered. In light of this, the only way in which trade can emerge is via specialized traders (merchants), who buy and sell goods. Assume, for the sake of argument, that a specialized trader deals in only one good, and makes payment in gold (stock). Further, assume that the relative price of each of the goods is unity. The question is whether, in a Nash setting, market exchange involving specialized traders will emerge spontaneously, that is without the presence of a third party (government, coordinating agent, etcetera).

Consider, to begin with, the no-trade case. That is, there are no specialized traders. The question is, will trade (intermediated) emerge? Let us examine the potential specialized trader's problem. To enter the market (so to speak), s/he must purchase a unit of good i, and pay for it in terms of gold. The problem, however, is on the revenue side. If s/he is the only trader, then there is little chance of selling good i, for lack of income (in this case, gold). The producer of good i has no interest in buying it back. Thus, in a Nash setting, there are no incentives to "make a market," so to speak. We refer to this result as *The Spontaneous Private Market Impossibility Theorem*." If spontaneous market trade is impossible, then it is unclear whether specialization will emerge. Put differently, if agents cannot sell and buy in organized markets, then there will be no incentive to specialize.

It follows that only if at least two potential specialized traders can communicate and, as a result, coordinate their activities can markets as defined here emerge. The emergence of markets is analogous to a prisoner's dilemma. Without coordination, markets organized around specialized traders cannot emerge. Examples of successful coordination in the past include the presence of public choice mechanisms (i.e. government expenditure), which, as shown earlier in this chapter, "makes the market," thus circumventing the prisoner's dilemma.

The Spontaneous Private Market Impossibility Theorem, we maintain, can be used to explain the absence of non-government market activity organized around specialized traders, and private money, in antiquity and in the pre-industrial revolution period—the Polanyi hypothesis (attributed to Karl Polanyi). Making the market, by which is meant trading gold for goods with an eye to resale, is a public good. The gold (money, credit) received by the vendor (producer) is a public good as soon as s/he begins to spend it. The vendor cannot appropriate all of it for him/herself. As with all public goods, there is the risk of undersupply.

Appendix II: A Descriptive Account of Royal Merchant Trade

This appendix presents a brief descriptive account of royal merchant trade, which, as we argue, marks the beginning of markets, money and organized (intermediated) trade. Consider an environment in which there are n producers, one merchant, and one sovereign. Suppose that owing to the presence of belligerent tribes on the border of the kingdom, the sovereign must maintain a standing army, prepared at all times to defend his subjects—and his property. Suppose also that the total product of the kingdom is 100 *roi*'s, *roi*'s being the unit of account, and that the cost of a standing army is ten *roi*'s.

As pointed out earlier, the sovereign has two choices. Either he collect ten *roi*'s worth of output with which to pay his army in kind, or establish a system of money, merchants and taxes (monetary). If he opts for the former, then he incurs the cost of a bureaucracy, whose purpose is to collect, store, and transport the ten *roi*'s of goods and services needed to defend the kingdom. If he chooses the latter, then he issues currency (coinage) in the amount of ten *roi*'s, which is declared legal tender, and is paid to the army. The soldiers use the money to purchase goods and service. Furthermore, it is decreed that all taxes must, heretofore, be paid in *roi*'s. Taxpayers, in turn, must sell goods and services to the soldiers, or sell goods and services to those who sold goods and services to soldiers, etcetera. In all likelihood, specialized merchants will spontaneously arise, purchasing goods and services from individuals and paying in money (i.e. *roi*'s).

More importantly, as taxes are now payable in *roi*'s, it stands to reason that the initial ten *roi*'s worth of trade will engender, via a multiplier-like process, more monetary trade, as citizens not dealing directly with the sovereign (or his merchants) will have to somehow acquire *roi*'s with which to honor their outstanding tax liability. Should the economy not be producing at capacity, one could argue that such expenditure would increase wealth. Perhaps similar considerations were what prompted mercantilists to argue that wealth was increasing in bullion.

3

The Fordization of America

The story of mass production at the Ford Motor Company was not some-thing that only historians of a later generation would delve into and try to understand. Henry Ford's contemporaries, many of whom were com-petitors, closely watched the doings at Highland Park, attempting to understand and emulate the revolutionary developments. Henry Ford encouraged their interest. Unlike the Singer Manufacturing Company, the Ford Company was completely open about its organizational struc-ture, its sales, and its production methods.... As a consequence of Ford's openness, Ford production technology diffused rapidly throughout Ameri-can manufacturing.

—David Hounshell, *From the American System to Mass Production*

Economic historians agree that energy-based innovations were instrumen-tal in the rise of Western civilization. According to Nathan Rosenberg and L. E. Birdzell, Jr., the West's ability to harness and exploit the earth's abundant supply of energy figures among the principal causes of its phenomenal growth.[1] In this chapter, we begin by examining in detail what is regarded as the most significant process innovation of the 20th century, namely the electri-fication of manufacturing activity and the resulting extremely-high-through-put, continuous-flow mass production processes. The focus will, as such, be on the first major application of electric power in U.S. manufacturing which occurred at the Ford Motor Company's Highland Park plant in a suburb of Detroit. While Henry Ford was not the first to use electricity, he and his team

51

of engineers were, nonetheless, the first to see and profitability exploit the numerous process-based applications, the end result of which was extremely-high-throughput, continuous-flow production techniques (hereafter EHTCFPT), commonly referred to as mass production. Inanimate energy replaced animate energy, resulting in record increases in conventionally-defined productivity.

In little time, news of the phenomenal successes at the Ford Motor Company's Highland Park plant spread throughout the automobile industry, and throughout U.S. industry. In 1929, the electrification of U.S. industry was identified as the "single most important change in U.S. industry" by the President's *Conference on Unemployment* chaired by Herbert C. Hoover.

> Characteristic also has been the rise in the use of power-three and three-quarters times faster than the growth of population-and the extent to which power has been made readily available not alone for driving tools of increased size and capacity, but for a convenient diversity of purposes in the smallest business enterprise and on the farm and in the home. Factories no longer need to cluster about the source of power. Widespread interconnection between power plants, arising out of an increasing appreciation of the value of flexibility in power and made possible by technical advances during recent years, has created huge reservoirs of power so that abnormal conditions in one locality need not stop the wheels of industry. The increasing flexibility with which electricity can be delivered from power has enabled manufacturers and farmers to meet high labor costs by the application of power-driven specialized machines; and power in this flexible form has penetrated into every section of the United States, including many rural areas. The survey shows that as a nation we now use as much electricity as all the rest of the world combined. Through the subdivision of power, the unskilled worker has become a skilled operator, multiplying his effectiveness with specialized automatic machinery and processes. (National Bureau of Economic Research 1929, *xi*)

Warren D. Devine, Jr. described the shift from steam to electric power as the most rapid and complete transitions in energy use in history:

> Perhaps the most rapid and complete transition in energy use was the shift from steam power to electric power for driving machinery. Steam power prevailed at the turn of the century, with steam engines providing around 80 percent of total capacity for driving machinery. By 1920 electricity had replaced steam as the major source of motive power, and by 1929-just

forty-five years after their first use in a factory-electric motors provided 78 percent of all mechanical drive. (Devine 1990, 21)

Richard B. Du Boff described it as: "Probably the most sweeping and complex technological change in American manufacturing over the past century has been electrification" (1967, 510).

The second part of the chapter will examine the spread of electric power throughout U.S. industry and its macroeconomic consequences. We will be particularly interested in its effects on aggregate productivity, income and expenditure. Did the U.S. economy grow faster as predicted by equilibrium growth theory? Did real wages reflect the increased productivity? It will be shown that income (nominal and real) and output failed to increase in response to higher productivity. Real wages over the course of the 1920s remained relatively constant, confirming what Henry Ford and Boston merchant Edward A. Filene maintained throughout this period, namely that income, particularly wage income, had failed to keep pace with productivity.

The Early U.S. Auto Industry

At the turn of the century, the nascent U.S. automobile industry consisted of a dozen small firms, scattered geographically throughout the industrialized Northeast. The Pope Manufacturing Company in Hartford, Connecticut, produced the Pope-Tribune, the Pope-Hartford, the Pope-Robinson, the Pope-Waverly, and the Pope-Toledo. Winton, Stearns, and Packard were located in Ohio. The Pierce Automobile Company was located in Buffalo, while the American Automobile Company was located in Massachusetts. Detroit had the Ford Motor Company, Buick, Northern, Reliance and the Mohawk. According to Ford biographer Allan Nevins (1954), "Expansion, exuberant and often reckless, was a dominant characteristic of the early industry" (Nevins 1954, 222). Entry and exit were commonplace. According to Nevins: "New companies seemed to spring to life daily. Many like the Century, the Waltham, the Overman, and the Mohawk would soon fall by the wayside; others would endure. But the birthrate was astounding and the death rate high" (Nevins 1954, 222).

Among these upstart firms was the Ford Motor Company, located in Detroit, Michigan, founded by a former engineer at the Detroit Edison Illuminating Company, Henry Ford. Born and raised in nearby Dearborn in 1886 at age 25, he left the family farm. Being mechanically inclined, he found work at the Detroit Edison Illuminating Company as a night engineer.[2] Founded and owned by Thomas Edison, the Detroit Edison Illuminating Company provided power to the city of Detroit and surrounding areas. In little time, he was promoted to chief engineer, a position he would keep until he left in 1899. It could be argued that his experience at the Detroit Edison Illuminating Company played a key role in his later successes as the founder and president of the world's largest automobile manufacturer.

According to Ford biographers, during this period he devoted his leisure hours to various mechanical pursuits. One such pursuit was the horseless carriage. Buoyed by the success of Europeans, specifically the Germans and the French, countless young U.S. mechanics tried their hand at building horseless carriages. In 1895, while still at the Detroit Edison Illuminating Company, he built his first vehicle, the "quadricycle." Encouraged, in 1899 he quit his job and devoted himself entirely to the automobile. In 1903, he established the Ford Motor Company.

Ease of entry into the U.S. auto industry, owing to what were minimal capital costs, made the all firms, including the Ford Motor Company vulnerable. Competition was fierce. In its first decade, the Ford Motor Company, in the image and likeness of its president, produced a number of different models, each with a different price. Among these were the *Model A*, the *Model B*, the *Model C* and the *Model F*, all of which retailed for between $1,000 and $2,000. Ford's automobiles were competitively priced—the Pope-Hartford sold for $3,200, and the Packard sold for $7,000.

At the time, the average daily wage in U.S. manufacturing was between $2.00 and $2.50. Average annual manufacturing income stood at $750, or one-third the price of Ford's *Model B* ($2,000), and nearly one-quarter the price of the Pope-Hartford. As such, the automobile was a luxury item, out of the reach of the average American worker and farmer. Ford realized that unless the industry could produce a quality, well-built, and affordable automobile, its future would be limited. This ultimately led to the Model T, the quintessential affordable, durable, and reliable automobile.

Beginning in 1903, Ford and his engineers set their sights on a single goal, reducing cost. As cost savings could only be achieved by increasing volume, Ford constantly sought to increase output. When existing facilities and layouts proved to be unworkable, he relocated. in 1904, the manufacturing end of operations was transferred to the new Piquette Street plant. in the first year, 1,745 cars were produced. While an improvement over the former Mack

Street plant, it failed to address all of Ford's concerns, especially regarding sequential production.

According to Ford biographers, it was at this point in time that Ford and his engineers soured on static assembly techniques. According to Nevins:

> That Ford, Wills and their aides were acutely aware of the disadvantages of this old-style procedure is unquestionable. No continuity of manufacture existed, the order of work suffering constant interruption. To be sure, an effort was made to preserve a certain neatness; parts were never dumped loose on the floor, but brought up in wooden boxes, white wheels were kept at the side of frames and rolled over as needed. Nevertheless, looking at the unsystematic, cluttered rooms, Ford and his chief associates began to ponder a better arrangement: a plan by which machines, employees, and materials should be placed in a sequential line of production. (Nevins 1954, 267)

Most observers view sequential production (i.e. mass production) as Ford's seminal contribution to manufacturing processes. in fact, to most, Henry Ford and sequential production are synonymous. Sequential production, we argue, had little to do with his success, and, in fact, as Hounshell (1984) points out, predated the Ford Motor Company by at least a century. Rather, Ford's contribution lies in the application of power to the idea of sequence. in other words, applying electric power to conveyor belts and all other forms of sequential production.

THE ELECTRIFICATION OF THE ASSEMBLY LINE

Ford's early attempts at sequential production were moderately successful. Workers or gravity would push the various parts and products along the "assembly line." Productivity increased, but only marginally. Sometime and somewhere between the gravity—and worker-activated assembly lines that characterized the Piquette Street plant and the first assembly line (i.e. magneto assembly line), Ford and his engineers realized that productivity could be increased and costs decreased by applying electromagnetic power to sequential processes. The result is what we refer to as extremely-high-throughput, continuous-flow production techniques (EHTCFPT's). The key was electric power. Clearly, his years at the Detroit Edison Illuminating Company played a key role role in this seminal technological breakthrough. Productivity could be greatly increased if parts, rather than workers moved.

"Every piece of work in the shop moves. It may move on hooks, on overhead chains…it may travel on a moving platform, or it may go by gravity, but the point is there is no lifting or trucking. No workman has anything to do with moving or lifting anything. Let the conveyor do the walking. Save ten steps a day for each of the 12,000 employees, and you will have saved fifty miles of wasted motion and misspent energy. (Lacey 1986, 109)

Ford's genius consisted of applying a new, versatile power source (i.e. electricity) to the well-known and well-used techniques of interchangeable parts and sequential production.[3] According to David Hounshell, interchangeable parts and the assembly line can both be traced back to the nineteenth century. Interchangeable parts were instrumental in the growth of the French and U.S. armaments industries. The assembly line had characterized a number of nineteenth-century U.S. industries including the Westinghouse Foundry, the Singer Sewing Machine Company, and various Midwestern slaughterhouses.[4]

The world's first moving assembly line came in the spring of 1913, in the magneto department at Highland park. Workers, lined up side by side, facing the flywheels designed by Spider Huff. These flywheels rested on waist-high metal shelving along which the components could be slid, and below the shelf, each man had a bin containing just one or two components…. When the waist-level shelving was replaced by a rather more elevated, motorized conveyor belt which set the pace for the line, production time fell even more…. Stopwatches went into action. An analysis of production at Highland Park that August showed 250 assemblers and 80 parts carriers working nine hours each day for twenty-six days to complete 6,182 chassis and motors-an average of twelve and a half man-hours per chassis. As an experiment, a crude moving line was set up with a rope running 250 feet down the factory from one chassis to a winch which hauled the rope in slowly across the floor. As the chassis moved, a group of six assemblers kept pace with it, picking up parts as they needed them from strategic dumps along the way-and 10 and behold, the average number of man-hours needed to complete a chassis fell to five hours and fifty minutes. (Lacey 1986, 134)

Productivity soared. in 1912, 82,388 Model Ts were produced with 6,867 employees. in 1913, output more than doubled to 189,088 Model Ts as did employees at 14,366. However, the following year, output climbed to 230,788 Model Ts with fewer employees, 12,880. in 1915, with EHTCFPT's, output soared to 394,788. in the 1926 edition of the *Encyclopaedia Britannica*, Ford described mass production as follows:

Mass production is not merely quantity production, for this may be had with none of the requisites of mass production. Nor is it merely machine production, which also may exist without any resemblance to mass production. Mass production is the focusing upon a manufacturing project of the principles of power, accuracy, economy, system, continuity, and speed. (Ford 1926a, 821)

The operative word here is power, from which all else (e.g., accuracy, economy, system, continuity and speed) derived. Put differently, system, continuity, and speed are by-products of the electrification/automation of sequential production. Power was at the core of the revolution that was mass production. The years Ford had spent at the Detroit Edison Illuminating Company (1886-1899) had paid handsome dividends.

Figure 3.1
Ford Motor Company Production Data, 1909-1916

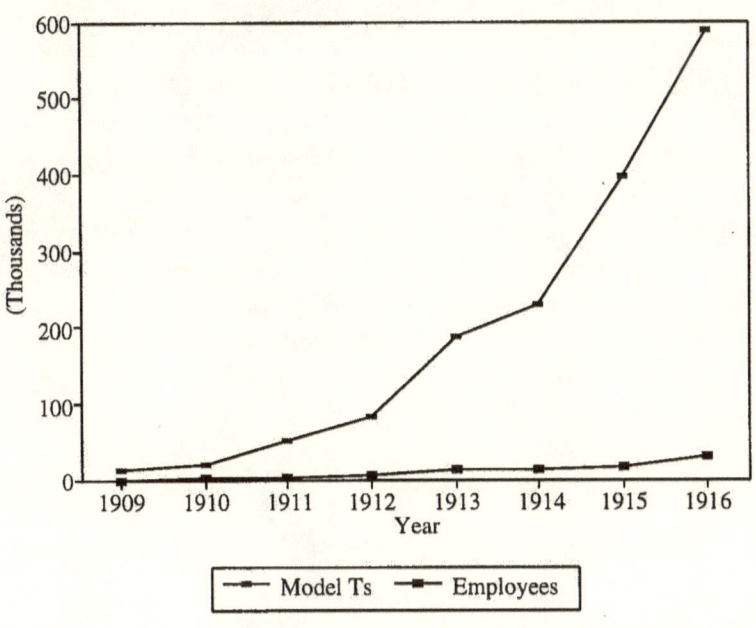

Source: Beaudreau (1996), 6.

The outcome went on to define EHTCFPT. Conventionally-measured labor productivity soared. in his autobiography, Ford provided a detailed accounts of the use of power at the Highland Park plant (i.e. leading to EHTCFPT's). Prior to 1913, with static assembly techniques (i.e. work stations), 20 minutes of labor were required to assemble a magneto. With production reorganized around an electric-powered conveyor belt, 13 minutes-10 seconds, 7 minutes, and finally, 5 minutes of labor were required (see Table 3.1). For transmissions, it decreased from 18 minutes to 9 minutes, 12 seconds. For the overall Model-T chassis, it decreased from 12 hours, 28 minutes, to 6 hours, and finally to 1 hour, 33 minutes (Ford 1922, 81). Expressed in terms of productivity growth rates, these yield increases in the order of 300 percent in the case of magneto assembly, 100 percent in the case of transmission assembly, and 1,100 percent in the case of chassis assembly.

Table 3.1
Ford Motor Company Productivity-Assembly Processes *

Process	Phase	Assembly Time	Index
Magneto	Initial	20 minutes	100
	I	13 minutes, 10 seconds	66
	II	7 minutes	35
	III	5 minutes	25
Transmission Cover	Initial	18 minutes	100
	I	9 minutes	50
Chassis Assembly	Initial	12 hours, 28 minutes	100
	I	6 hours	48
	II	1 hour, 33 minutes	12

*   Source: Beaudreau (1996), 6.

Output at the Highland Park plant increased at astounding rates. Referring to Figure 3.1, we see that 13,840 Model Ts were produced in 1909, with a combined labor force of 1,655 employees. By 1915, 394,788 were produced with a labor force of 18,892 employees. Over this six-year period, the number of Model Ts per employee went from eight in 1909 to 14 in 1911 and to an astounding 20 in 1915 (see Figure 3.2). Percentage-wise, productivity increased 150 percent.

Figure 3.2
Ford Motor Company Labor Productivity Data, 1909-1916

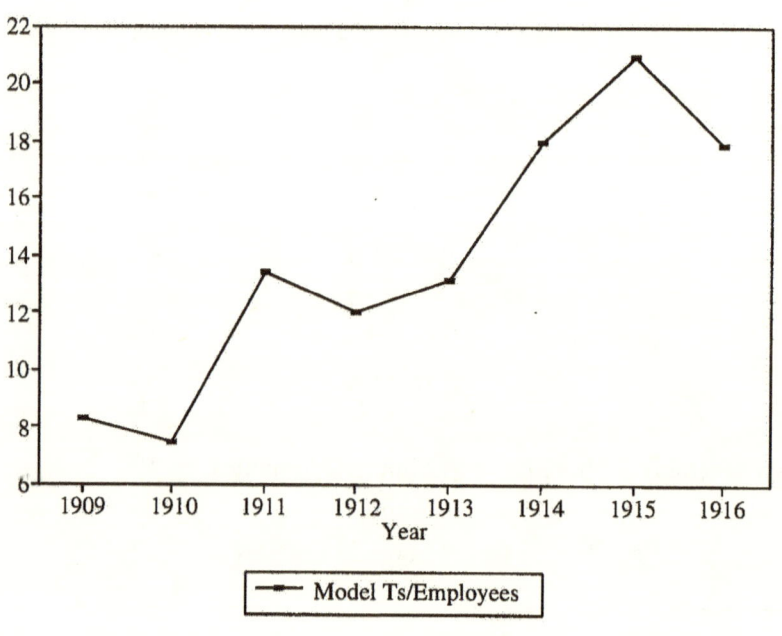

Source: Beaudreau (1996), 7.

At the center of this *miracle* was inanimate energy in the form of electric power. The Highland Park plant was literally and figuratively built around a 3,000-horsepower gas engine that turned direct-current generating equipment.[5] According to Hounshell: "Power was distributed throughout the factory by electric motors which drove units of line shafting and belting. When Colvin visited the factory (1913) construction was nearing completion on an additional five thousand-horsepower gas engine" (Hounshell 1984, 229).[6]

Wage Policy at the Ford Motor Company

How did workers at the Ford Motor Company fare in what ranks as one of the greatest technological and economic watersheds in modern history? Did they share in the new-found source of wealth (electric power)? Did wages increase commensurately with productivity? As it turns out, one of, if not the, most enigmatic decisions taken by Henry Ford as president and chief operating officer of the Ford Motor Company was to double wages. in 1913, the average wage at the Ford Motor Company had stood at $2.43 per day (10-hour day). On January 17, 1914, the Board of Directors, under pressure from Ford himself, approved a new wage scale that set the minimum wage at $5.00.

What prompted Ford to unilaterally double wages? To this very day, scholars continue to debate the reasons which led him to double his payroll. Ford biographers and scholars have studied this question at length. Among the reasons commonly advanced are (*i*) encroaching trade unionism (*ii*) high rates of labor turnover, and (*iii*) Ford's concern for the plight of his workers. Some have argued that Ford, by doubling wages, thwarted attempts by union organizers to gain entry into the FMC. Others have pointed to what appear to be abnormally high rates of worker turnover. Ford biographer Allan Nevins, on the other hand, points to Ford's beneficent paternalism.[7] As we saw above, productivity in the period 1912-1914 had risen sharply, earnings had risen to record heights, dividends had risen, management salaries had risen; why should workers not share in the success, asked Ford? According to Nevins:

> The net income [of FMC] went from $4 millions in the calendar year 1910, above $7 millions in 1911 and above $13.5 million in 1913. Dividends declared during 1913 aggregated $15.2 million. As Ford and Couzens became colossally rich, as they paid their executives higher and higher salaries and bonuses, and as they gave the public cheaper and cheaper cars, they had to ask themselves: what of our workers? Was it fair of a corporation which by 1913 had more than $28 millions in surplus to keep paying Tom Smith and Carlo Pastucci only $2.00 to $2.50 a day? (Nevins 1954, 527)

In the following chapters, it will be argued that the five, six (1919) and seven-dollar day (1932) were more than beneficent paternalism on the part of Henry Ford; rather, they defined, and thus were consistent with, his lifelong views on wages, income, economic growth and progress. Specifically, using various sources, it will be shown that the five-dollar day in 1914, the six-dollar day in 1919 and the seven-dollar day in 1933 were Ford, the social analyst's, visionary response to the problem of technology shock-based underincome.

Figure 3.3
Ford Motor Company Wage and Price Indexes, 1909-1916

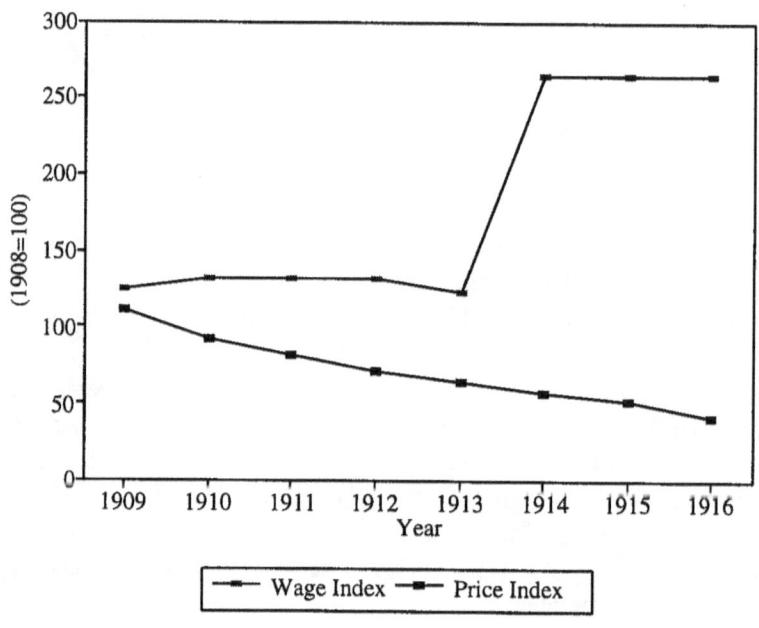

Source: Beaudreau (1996), 9.

PRICING POLICY AT THE FORD MOTOR COMPANY

While the five-dollar day was a radical departure from the commonly accepted wage-setting practices (i.e. paying the going rate), Ford's pricing policies were nonetheless consistent with the basic principles of competition: continually lower prices in the hope of increasing market share, revenue, earnings, and dividends. As indicated, Ford was driven by a singular goal: make the best possible automobile at the lowest possible price. The record shows that he remained faithful to this credo. Referring to Figure 3.3, we see that from 1909 onward, the price of the Model T decreased monotonically. in 1909, it stood at $950; by 1912, it had fallen to $600, a 37 percent price decrease. By 1916, it stood at $360, which corresponds to a 62 percent price decrease relative to 1909.

Clearly, Ford had achieved the goal he had set in the early 1910s, namely to build an affordable automobile. At $360, the average American worker, earning roughly $750 per year, had the means to buy a Model T. By 1926, 15 million Model Ts had been sold.

The Fordization of America

The electrification of the assembly line at the Ford Motor Company's Highland Park plant radically altered the U.S. automobile industry. Work would never be the same. Electric power would go on to play an increasingly important role in the U.S. manufacturing industry. Conventionally-measured productivity soared as did output. By 1916, the Highland Park plant was turning out over a half-million Model Ts, a miracle by any account. At the center of this miracle lay electric power. The Ford Motor Company in the 1910s was a microcosm of the U.S. economy in the 1920s. Overall productivity and output increased; employment, however, remained relatively constant. in this section, we examine various aspects of electrification à la Ford on aggregate U.S. productivity.

THE ELECTRIFICATION OF THE ASSEMBLY LINE AS A TECHNOLOGY SHOCK

The electrification of the assembly line is an example of what has become known as a general purpose technology (Bresnahan and Trajtenberg 1992; Helpman and Trajtenberg 1994). As David Hounshell pointed out, the techniques developed at the FMC were diffused rapidly throughout the U.S. economy and indeed throughout the Western world. It therefore follows that the electrification of the assembly line provides us with a unique opportunity to examine, in detail, the many aspects of a technology shock. With this in mind, we examine both the spread, and the effects on macroeconomic aggregates, of this revolutionary process technology throughout and on American industry. To begin with, we focus on the rate at which U.S. manufacturing firms adopted the production techniques developed by Ford and his engineers at the Ford Motor Company's Highland Park plant. This raises a number of problems, not the least of which was that of finding a suitable measure of the relevant diffusion process. How does one measure the spread of EHTCFPT? Another problem was the paucity of aggregate and disaggregated data for the 1920s. As it turns out, most aggregate series start in 1929.

This turned out to be less of a problem than anticipated. EHTCFPT, unlike previous energy-intensive process innovations (i.e. the advent of steam-powered machinery), was not embodied in tools or machinery. Instead, it consisted of a radical reorganization of the production process around a new energy source, namely electric power.

> The focus in the organization of production changed from a primary emphasis on achieving economies of scale to a growing attention to the opportunity to accelerate the flow of throughput within the factory. Major advances came about as a result of the introduction of electrical systems for distributing power within the plant in place of earlier steam-based systems for power distribution. (Sonenblum 1990, 279)

Existing machinery, equipment, and workers were simply rearranged along an electric-powered conveyor belt; this was known as the assembly line.

> It is found that the output of manufacturing establishments is materially increased in most cases by the use of electric driving. It is often found that the gain actually amounts to 20 to 30 percent or even more, with the same floor space, machinery, and number of workmen. This is the most important advantage of all because it secures an increase in income without an increase in investment, labor or expense, except perhaps for material. in many cases, the output is raised and at the same time the labor item is reduced. (Devine 1990, 32)

Time-series data on plant and equipment are, as such, of limited use. The key element (input) in this revolutionary technique as developed by Ford was energy-specifically, electric power. Firms substituting conventional static work (assembly) stations with EHTCFPTs would increase their use of electric power. Time-series data on industrial electric power consumption can, as such, serve as a proxy for the diffusion of mass production (EHTCFPT).

Figure 3.4
U.S. Electric Power Consumption per Worker—Manufacturing,
1912-1945

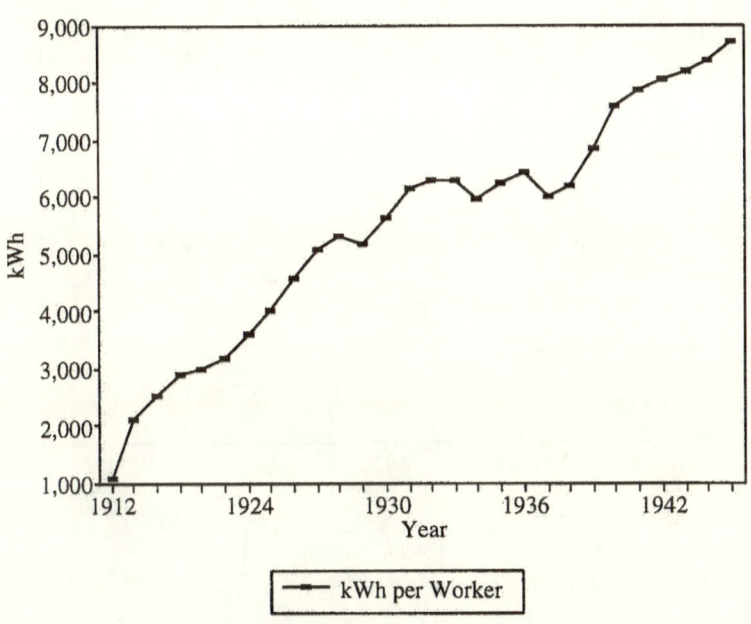

Source: Beaudreau (1996), 12.

Figure 3.5
U.S. Total Electric Power Consumption—Manufacturing, 1912-1945

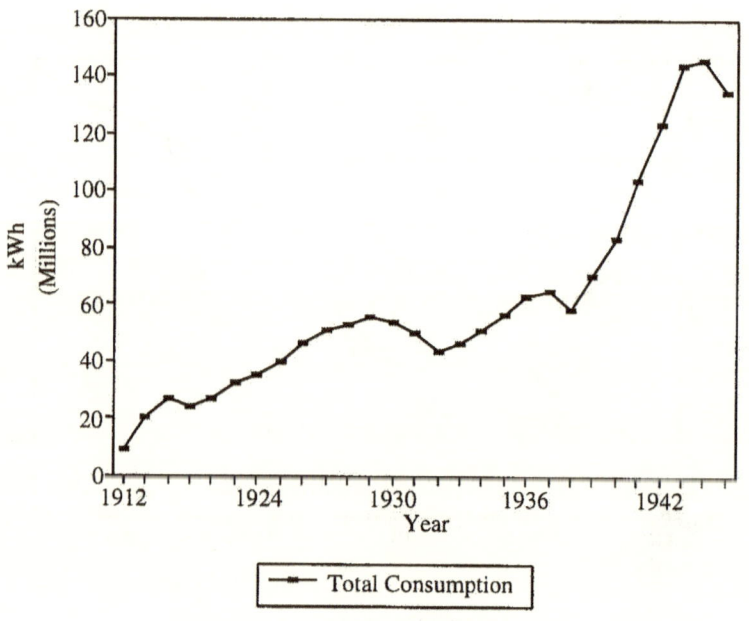

Source: Beaudreau (1996), 15.

Using data obtained from the U.S. Department of Commerce's *Historical Statistics of the United States* on electric power consumption and employment in manufacturing, a diffusion index for EHTCFPT was constructed. Referring to Figure 3.4, electric power consumption per employee in 1918 stood at 2,101 kilowatt hours per annum in 1918. By 1920, it had increased by 25 percent, to 2,514 kilowatt hours; by 1926, it had more than doubled to 4,563 kilowatt-hours. American manufacturing was rapidly *Fordizing*. Total electric power consumption in manufacturing (see Figure 3.5) increased sixfold from 1912 to 1930, from 9,250 to 53,930 million kilowatt hours.

The index was constructed as follows. To begin with, it was assumed that by 1944, the electrification of U.S. industry as defined by EHTCFPT was complete.[8] Base year (1944) consumption of electric power per manufacturing employee stood at 8,368 kilowatt hours per employee per annum (see Table 3.1). Nineteen years earlier (1925), it stood at 3,995 kilowatt hours. Comparing these, we can infer that by 1925, EHTCFPT—the Fordization of U.S. manufacturing—was 48 percent complete. By 1930, it was 67 percent complete.

Table 3.2
U.S. Electric Power Consumption Diffusion Index-Manufacturing,
1920-1944 [*]

Year	ELEC/N	Index
1920	2,514	0.300
1921	2,904	0.347
1922	2,997	0.358
1923	3,158	0.377
1924	3,614	0.431
1925	3,995	0.477
1926	4,563	0.545
1927	5,103	0.609
1928	5,300	0.633
1929	5,150	0.615
1930	5,640	0.673
1931	6,170	0.737
1932	6,276	0.750
1933	6,294	0.752
1934	5,951	0.711
1935	6,252	0.747
1936	6,405	0.765
1937	5,999	0.716
1938	6,191	0.739
1939	6,861	0.819
1940	7,580	0.905
1941	7,886	0.942
1942	8,034	0.960
1943	8,180	0.977

Table 3.2
U.S. Electric Power Consumption Diffusion Index-Manufacturing,
1920-1944 (Continued)*

1944	8,368	1.000

---

*   kilowatt hours
Source: Beaudreau (1996), 16.

Electric Power and Manufacturing Productivity

How did EHTCFPT's affect manufacturing productivity? Did productivity in U.S. manufacturing jump by 100 percent across the board? Throughout this period, anecdotal references to the effects of electric power on manufacturing productivity were commonplace. For example, Chicago power magnate Martin J. Insull declared that "as a consequence of the added power which invention has contributed to industry, the forty-five and one-half million workers in the United States have achieved an output equivalent to from six-hundred million to nine-hundred million workers before the power era" (Fisher 1930, 131). This translates into a 1,300 percent increase in productivity.

Another power zealot, Matthew S. Sloan (president of the New York Edison Company), in a speech delivered at the annual dinner of trust companies in Chicago in February 1929, described the effects of electric power on productivity.

> Mr. Sloan compared this age which he termed the 'new industrial revolution' with 'the industrial revolution' in the eighteenth century, when the steamboat and locomotive came into use. As steam brought in the machine era, electricity, he said, has brought in the era of mass production which has so greatly affected the general economic situation and social conditions. Thus, electricity, he said, is responsible for our present production. With all its attendant circumstances of lowered unit costs, lowered prices, increased wages, intensified merchandising, wider markets, higher standard of living. Electricity-motivating machinery has multiplied the working power of the nation many times, he said, and the generating stations of the country now have a capacity of 35,000,000 horsepower, or the ability to do the work of about 350,000,000 men. in 1900, the generating capacity was only 3,000,000 horsepower.[9]

To gauge the effect of electric power on productivity, the *National Bureau of Economic Research* (NBER) index of output per man-hour was plotted against electric power consumption per worker in manufacturing from 1920 to 1944. Referring to Figure 3.6, output per man-hour in 1920 stood at 32, while electric power per worker stood at 2,514 kilowatt hours per annum. By 1944, electric power consumption in manufacturing had increased 232 percent, from 2,514 kilowatt hours per annum in 1920 to 8,368 kilowatt hours per annum in 1944. Output per man-hour in manufacturing in this period increased from 32 to 72. Except for the period 1930-1937, the level of output per man-hour was monotonically increasing in the level of electric power consumption per worker.

From 1920 to 1929, electric power consumption per worker increased 104 percent, from 2,514 to 5,150 kilowatt hours per annum. in this same period, output per man-hour increased 62 percent, from 32 to 52 (NBER labor productivity index). This is consistent with Beaudreau (1995, 1998) who reported output elasticities for electric power in the 0.53 to 0.63 range. In other words, a one percent increase in electric power consumption will increase manufacturing output/output per employee anywhere from 0.53 to 0.63 percent.

Figure 3.6
U.S. Electric Power Consumption-Productivity-Manufacturing,
1920-1945

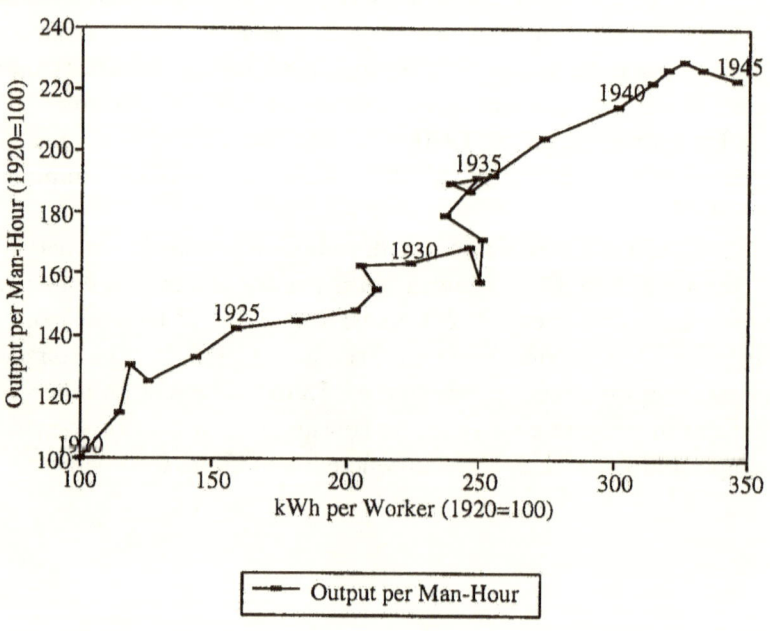

Source: U.S. Department of Commerce (1975), series 0802, 0130, S124.

Mass Production and Agriculture

The Fordization of America had a profound impact on the agricultural sector, one that is often glossed over in work on EHTCFPT's and mass production, one that was twofold, consisting of a direct impact and an indirect impact. The direct impact came as the result of the introduction of the gasoline-powered tractor (Fordson, Ferguson and International Harvestor), which increased yields markedly. Counting production by all manufacturers in the United States, 133,000 tractors were built in 1918—of those, *Ford and Son Tractor Company* sold 34,167 of them. By 1923 *Fordson* had captured 77% of the market with more than 100,000 tractors sold. Farm productivity increased substantially.

The introduction of the internal combustion engine, however, did more than increase farm productivity: it decreased the derived demand for hay and cereal on the part of the animal-based transportation sector. With the advent of the automobile and truck, not to mention the tractor, horses and oxen as prime movers were phased out, reducing the demand for farm produce.

> On balance, however, the tractor has had a markedly positive economic impact. Horses and mules, while providing farm power, ate up more than twenty percent of the food they helped farmers grow! By replacing them with machines that consumed much less expensive quantities of fuel, oil, and hydraulic fluid, farmers were able to reduce their costs and pass these social savings along to food buyers. More importantly, the millions of farm workers freed up by the technology were able to contribute their labor elsewhere in the economy, creating large economic benefits. According to a recent estimate by the author, the U.S. would have been almost ten percent poorer in 1955 in the absence of the farm tractor. Along with the revolution in yields generated by the advances in biological and chemical research, the farm tractor has helped agriculture make a significant contribution to economic growth in the United States. (White 2000, 56)

The combined effect of these was catastrophic. U.S. agriculture was more productive than ever. Yields per acre soared; however, demand for agricultural products was on the wane, owing to the growing use of fossil fuels.

The Literature on Mass Production

Throughout this period, productivity growth records were being shattered monthly, if not weekly. U.S. industry was in the throes of a revolution, the effects of which were as—if not more—important as those resulting from the introduction of the steam engine.[10] Yet, economists showed surprisingly little interest in what was an epoch-defining technology shock.

Businessmen (e.g. Henry Ford and Edward A. Filene) wrote extensively on the impact of mass production on the U.S. economy.[11] For example, Edward A. Filene, in *The Way Out: A Forecast of Coming Changes in American Business and Industry* (published in 1924) described in great detail the many changes in U.S. industry brought about by mass production. Chief among these was the *Fordization* of American business and industry. Seven years later, Filene, in collaboration with Charles W. Wood, published a second volume entitled *Successful Living in This Machine Age*. What is particularly noteworthy is the timing of this work, namely 1931. in the depths of the Great Depression,

Filene pleaded with his fellow industrialists to increase wages (see *Proposition 1* in Chapter 2).

Economists in general paid little attention to this radical process innovation. There were, however, some exceptions. For example, there was Professor Rexford G. Tugwell of Columbia University who examined the electrification of U.S. industry and its consequences. in a book entitled *Industry's Coming of Age* (1927), he described the "revolution underway in U.S. industry." Foremost among the "technical causes" of increased productivity, he argued, was "the bringing into use of new and better power resources more suited to our technique, more flexible and less wasteful; and continued progress in the technique of generating and applying power" (Tugwell 1927, 180)—in short, the electrification of U.S. industry.

> The electrification of industry has now progressed to the extent of between 55 and 60 per cent completion. So widespread an adoption of this new flexible means of moving things cannot have taken place without numerous secondary results in lowered costs, improvements in quality, and a heightened morale among workers. For the new power is not only cheaper to use; it is also cleaner, more silent and handier. On the whole, the electrification of industry must be set down as the greatest single cause of the new industrial revolution. (Tugwell 1927, 182)

What is remarkable about this literature (i.e. consisting of both professional and non-professional writings on electrification) is its dualistic (positive and normative) nature. in addition to providing detailed, anecdotal accounts of the impact of electric power on productivity and output, they examined the resulting problems. Chief among these was the problem of generalized excess capacity (see *Propositions 1* and *2* in Chapter 2). In short, America's capacity to produce had increased manifold; however, its ability to "take the products off of the market" had not, resulting in generalized excess capacity. Something had gone awry. To Ford and Filene, both successful businessmen, the cause was the prevailing business ethos: EHTCFPT-using firms systematically resisted wage increases (See *Propositions 1* and *2*) and/or price decreases. Mass production, they surmised, called for a fundamental change in wage and price setting behavior.[12]

> Mass production, it must be remembered, is not a system to be installed, with such and such appropriations for upkeep. It is a social revolution. It is production for the masses, for the first time in human history, and this is a form of production which, because of its constantly increasing capacity,

must, if understood and operated scientifically, abolish poverty and drudg-
ery and the fear of unemployment and all the discipline which has historically been founded upon these things. To operate this social mechanism
scientifically, however, requires more than just a formula in the possession
of a few great executives. It requires a new attitude toward society on the
part of business men and workers alike. (Filene 1931, 151)

An attempt to fill the void left by the economics profession was made by a
group of U.S pure and applied scientists, known collectively as the *Continental
Committee on Technocracy* (Scott 1933). With the declared purpose of "recog-
nizing the importance of the scientific method in the operation of a well-
ordered society," Technocracy was, in large measure, a response to the failure
on the part of the academic community in the United States, specifically the
economics profession, to acknowledge, examine, and understand the effects of
electrification on the U.S. economy.

A century ago these United States had a population of approximately
12,000,000, whereas today our census figures a total of 122,000,000—a ten-
fold increase in the century. One hundred years ago, in these United States,
we consumed less than 75 trillion British thermal units of extraneous energy
per annum, whereas in 1929 we consumed approximately 27,000 trillion British thermal units-an increase of 353 fold in the century. Our energy consumption now exceeds 150,000 kilogram calories per capita per day; whereas
in the year 1800 our consumption of extraneous energy was not less than
1600 or more than 2000 kilogram calories per capita per day.... The United
States of our forefathers, with 12,000,000 inhabitants, performed its necessary work in almost entire dependence upon the human engine, which, as its
chief means of energy conversion, was aided and abetted only by domestic
animals and a few water wheels. The United States today has over one billion
installed horsepower. in 1929, these engines of energy conversion, though
operated only to partial capacity, nevertheless had an output that represented
approximately 50 percent of the total work of the world. When one realizes
that the technologist has succeeded to such an extent that he is to-day capable
of building and operating engines of energy conversion that have nine million
times the output capacity of the average single human being working an eight
hour day, one begins to understand the importance of this acceleration,
beginning with man as the chief engine of energy conversion and culminating
with these huge extensions of his original one-tenth of a horse power. Then
add the fact that of this 9,000,000-fold acceleration 8,766,000 has occurred
since the year 1900. (Scott 1933, 42)

TROUBLE IN EDEN: CHRONIC OVERSUPPLY

This literature was, in large measure, a reaction to its shortcomings, not its virtues. For example, chronic oversupply was Edward A. Filene's *cause célèbre*. in his view, mass production had increased America's ability to produce without having increased its ability to consume. What was required was nothing less than a fundamental and far-reaching change in the then prevailing business ethos. Wages would have to rise and prices would have to fall.

> In the future a really big business success on the basis of mass production and mass distribution will be impossible except as it makes for both high wages and low prices.... Low wages and high prices manifestly cut down that widespread and sustained buying power of the masses without which mass production sooner or later defeats itself. in other words, the business man of the future must produce prosperous customers as well as saleable goods. He cannot think of business as an adventure in getting money from the masses of people who, in one way or another for which he has no responsibility, have got money from someone else. His whole business policy must look forward to creating great buying power among the masses. Otherwise mass production cannot succeed. The business man of the future must fill the pockets of the workers and consumers before he can fill his pockets. (Filene 1924, 201)

This theme runs throughout the writings of Filene, Ford, and others: higher production requires higher consumption and higher consumption requires higher wages and lower prices.[13] Analytically, the widespread application of EHTCFPT's throughout the U.S. economy violated Say's law, the cornerstone of mainstream macroeconomics. Say's law holds that supply automatically creates its own demand. Oversupply is as such impossible. Ford and Filene—businessmen by profession—disagreed: greater capacity does not create greater income, and, thus, greater demand.

While the *Continental Committee on Technocracy* hailed the coming of a new age, one founded on energy, its main concern was the widening gap between supply and demand. According to Howard Scott:

> Moreover, to maintain a balance between production and consumption, with the number of factors involved, requires qualitative calculations beyond the frontiers of arithmetic. And so the technologist does not blame the men of business, finance and politics for not doing what they are not prepared to do. But when he examines the arithmetical possible, the entire

system of financial business takes on the air of unreality; it becomes an impossible world of fairy-tale and magic. (Scott 1933, 33)

OVERSUPPLY: THE EVIDENCE

To what extent had productivity growth outstripped wage growth? To what extent had *Propositions 1* and *2* in Chapter 2 crippled the U.S. economy in the 1920s? Referring to Table 3.3, we see that manufacturing productivity as measured by the *National Bureau of Economic Research's* output per man-hour series increased 62 percent going from a value of 32 in 1920 to 52 in 1929. The nominal wage in manufacturing, however, remained constant. in 1920, it stood at $0.55, while in 1929, it stood at $0.56. The real manufacturing wage, defined as the ratio of the nominal wage to the consumer price level (1958=100), increased 31 percent over this period. Most of this increase, however, occurred in the depression of 1921, during which the price level fell from 65.4 to 50.1. Thus, despite non-negligible productivity gains, firms in general resisted wage increases and price decreases. From 1922 to 1925, the real wage in U.S. manufacturing remained relatively constant, corroborating *Proposition 1*.

Table 3.3
U.S. Wage and Productivity Data, 1920-1929 [*]

Year	Wage	CPI	Real Wage	Prod. Index	Wage Index
1920	0.55	54.60	0.84	100	100
1921	0.51	54.60	0.93	115	111
1922	0.48	50.10	0.95	130	113
1923	0.52	51.30	1.01	125	120
1924	0.54	51.20	1.05	133	125
1925	0.54	51.90	1.04	142	123
1926	0.54	51.10	1.05	145	125
1927	0.54	50.00	1.08	148	128
1928	0.56	50.80	1.10	155	131
1929	0.56	50.60	1.10	162	131

[*] Source: U.S. Department of Commerce (1975), series F31.

Wage and Price Policy at the Ford Motor Company: A New Ethos for American Business

Ford and Filene advocated across-the-board wage increases combined with across-the-board price decreases. This stood in direct contradiction with the prevalent business ethos, which called for lower wages and higher prices. Wage increases and price decreases, except at the FMC, were perceived as being anathema to profit maximization. Ford and Filene, however, disagreed: in the era of mass production, the level of profits was an increasing function of the level of costs (i.e. labor costs).

> Under mass production, however, the profit motive not only can be attached to the common welfare, but it cannot escape being so attached. Under mass production, attaching it to any other aim spells loss. There can be no profit in mass production unless the masses are also profiting thereby. The time has come, however, when the greatest total profits can be secured only through supplying the masses with the best values. So there is no war now between selfishness and unselfishness; the only war is between the traditional notion of where self-interest lies and the newly discovered truths of profit-making. (Filene 1931, 198)

Consider wages, prices and productivity at the Ford Motor Company from 1908 to 1916. Referring to Figure 3.4, we see that productivity defined as the number *of* Model Ts per employee, measured using a simple index *(1908=100),* increased substantially from 1908 to 1915, reaching 249 in 1915. The real wage at the FMC, defined as the average nominal wage deflated by the consumer price level, tracks productivity growth. in 1908, the average daily wage stood at $1.89; by 1915, it had reached $5.00. The consumer price index in this period increased from 27.6 to 32.1. As such, the real wage went from 100 in 1908 to 263 in 1915, which compares favorably with the increase in the productivity index.

A second real wage index was constructed, namely the FMC real wage in kind (i.e. in terms of Model Ts). in this case, the nominal wage was deflated by the price index for Model Ts. in 1908, the price *of* a Model T stood at $850; by 1915, it had been halved and stood at $440. The corresponding real wage index increased from an initial value of 100 in 1908 to a value *of* 509 in 1915, a 409 percent increase. That is, relative to 1908, FMC workers in 1915 would have quintupled their consumption of Model Ts. Clearly, Ford practiced what he preached.

Conclusion

The 1920s was a decade of paradoxes. Productivity and productive capacity soared, yet output grew only slightly above historical rates. EHTCFPT's had radically increased America's ability to transform raw materials into finished goods. Engineers heralded a new era of unlimited potential, based on a new, flexible and inexpensive form of energy. Businessmen could hardly contain their enthusiasm as electric power provided a cheap source of energy and, ultimately, profits. As Nathan Rosenberg pointed out: "The sharp rise in productivity in the American economy, in the years after World War 1, doubtless owed a great deal, both directly and indirectly, to the electrification of manufacturing" (1972, 162). In the next chapters, it will be argued that America's failure to convert productivity growth into output growth (owing to *Propositions 1* and *2* in Chapter 2) prompted a number of policy responses, ranging from Senator Reed Smoot's tariff initiative (designed to secure a larger share of the U.S. market for domestic firms) to President Franklin D. Roosevelt and Senator Robert F. Wagner's blueprint for a managed economy, namely the National Industrial Recovery Act of 1933.

4

The First Policy Response: The Smoot-Hawley Tariff Bill of 1929

This chapter examines the first policy response to the conditions of generalized oversupply that characterized the U.S. economy in the 1920s: the Smoot-Hawley Tariff Bill of 1929. The analysis begins with the first mention by Senator Reed Smoot of Utah of oversupply and overproduction as a major problem, and ends with an in-depth look at what was, by far, the single most important by-product of this policy initiative, namely, the stock market boom and crash of 1928-1929. It will be argued that the stock market boom of 1928-1929, which witnessed a 70 percent increased in stock prices increase, was, in large measure, a response on the part of rational forward-looking investors to the proposed tariff revisions and the anticipated higher earnings, profits, and dividends. From July 1928 to October 1929 stock prices tracked tariff-related news, beginning with Senator Reed Smoot's announcement of Republican Herbert C. Hoover's presidential election campaign platform in July 1928.

Evidence of Generalized Oversupply

Initial indications that the U.S. economy found itself in a position of generalized oversupply came in the month of March 1928 when Democratic Senator Robert F. Wagner of New York tabled a resolution calling for a detailed report into the problem of growing unemployment from Secretary of Labor, James John Davis.[1] House and Senate Democrats maintained that unemployment was worsening, contrary to President Calvin Coolidge who maintained that the U.S. economy was fundamentally sound. Two days later, on March 7, 1928, Senator Reed Smoot of Utah, the chairman of the powerful Senate Finance Committee and presidential candidate Herbert C. Hoover's chief economic strategist, refuted these allegations.

Figure 4.1
U.S. Exports and Imports, 1921-1930

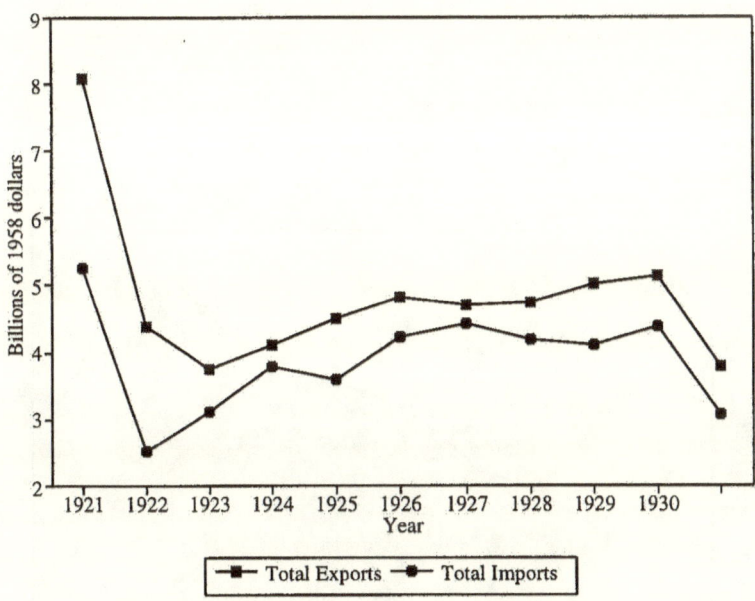

Source: U.S. Department of Commerce (1975), series U213, U219.

Senator Smoot insisted that the picture drawn by the Democrats on Monday, when the Senate passed the Senate resolution, was much overdrawn. He admitted that some unemployment existed, but insisted that it did not compare with that of 1920 and 1921 when the Republicans came into power after eight years of Democratic administration. As for one reason for a degree of unemployment, Senator Smoot referred to large importations of foreign merchandise which have been steadily reaching American shores in spite of the Republican protective tariff.... These imports have a tendency to supplant large quantities of American goods, despite the tariff, thus slowing down many American industries. There also was an over-supply or over-production in many lines, Senator Smoot contended, and over-production or under-consumption in the textiles industries.[2]

In the lengthy and highly acrimonious debate that followed, Senator Smoot referred repeatedly to mass production as a cause of overproduction.

A slow-down of many industries helps to increase industrial unemployment, and the result is immediately felt in the lowering of the consuming power of the wage earners. This has brought about what may be called an oversupply or overproduction existing in many lines; and I might add that mass production has cut a great figure in the amount of production in the United States in special lines.[3]

Figure 4.2
U.S. Exports and Imports of Manufactures, 1921-1930

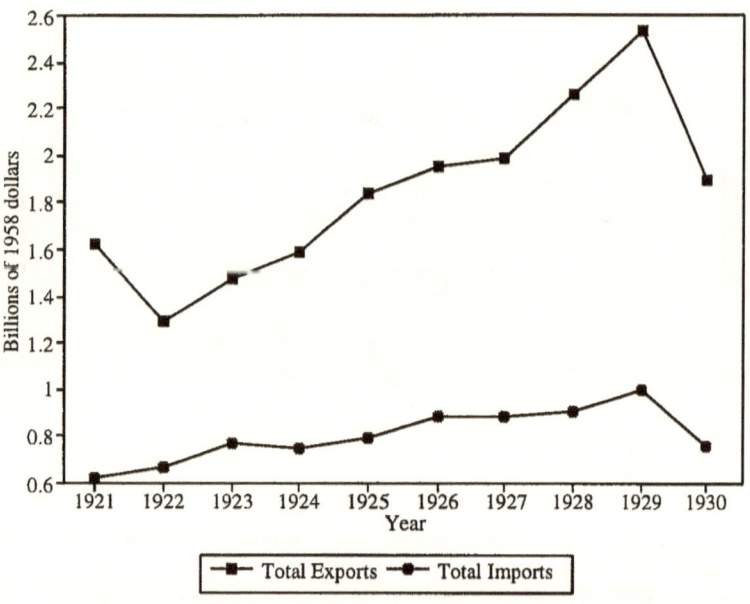

Source: U.S. Department of Commerce (1975), series U2I8, U224.

Out of this debate was to come the main plank of Republican Presidential hopeful, Herbert C. Hoover's, economic platform. Drafted by Old-Guard Republican Senator Reed Smoot, Hoover's "Kansas City platform" called for increased tariff protection and lower taxes.[4] Being the consummate politician he was, Smoot put the blame squarely on the shoulders of rising imports. Politically speaking, there was little to be gained from attributing it to the problem to mass production, to EHTCFPT's.

Figure 4.3
U.S. Exports and Imports of Food Products, 1921-1930

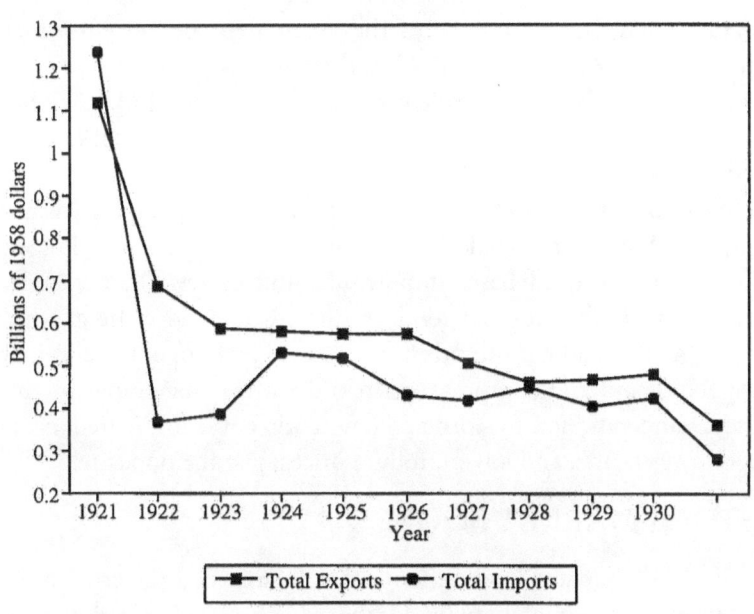

Source: Beaudreau (1996), 32.

The data for this period, however, fail to corroborate this, providing, instead, an altogether different picture of U.S. foreign trade in the 1920s. Throughout the 1920s, the United States ran a substantial trade account surplus. Referring to Figures 4.1-4.3 which present U.S. trade data from 1921 to 1930, U.S. exports exceeded U.S. imports. For example, in 1927, total exports stood at $4.759 billion and total imports at $4.185 billion. Exports of finished manufactures stood at $1.982 billion in 1927, dwarfing imports of $.879 billion. Moreover, exports of finished manufactures were growing faster than imports, the result of higher U.S. productivity. Such, however, was not the case for food products. Imports of food increased from 1921 to 1923, decreased from 1924 to 1926, and increased again from 1926 to 1927 before decreasing in 1928. Exports of food decreased from 1921 to 1927, and increased thereafter.

Thus, while U.S. imports of manufactures increased slightly from 1925 to 1928, U .S. exports of manufactures increased substantially. By 1928, the surplus on manufactures stood at $1.354 billion (constant 1958 dollars). As for food products, the data show that from 1922 to 1929, exports decreased. Imports decreased, but by less, with the result that the surplus which had stood at roughly $.20 billion in 1922 had been wiped out by 1927. On the whole, the overall U.S. foreign trade position was better in 1927 than in 1922. U.S. manufacturers had made significant inroad into foreign markets; imports remained the same.

Regardless, Senator Smoot remained categorical: excess capacity was due to rising imports. Something would have to be done. The policy of choice of the Republican party was tariff-based import substitution (see Chapter 1). Raising tariff rates on manufactures and food products would close the gap between productive capacity and consumption (i.e. reduce and hopefully eliminate the excess capacity), and, in the process, address the worsening employment problem. The Democrats, led by former New York governor Alfred E. Smith, advocated lower tariffs, and lower product prices, just the opposite.[5]

THE STOCK MARKET BOOM

On July 28, 1928, Senator Reed Smoot officially unveiled the economic plank of Republican presidential hopeful Herbert C. Hoover's election platform. Tariffs on both agricultural and manufactured goods would be raised and taxes would be lowered.[6] According to *The New York Times*:

> Upward revision of the tariff and another reduction in taxes by the next Congress if Secretary Hoover is elected President were predicted today by Senator Smoot, Chairman of the Finance Committee. Senator Smoot, who, as Chairman of the Resolutions Committee at the Kansas City Convention, drafted the tariff plank, said today that the Republican Party in this plank had promised not only upward revision of the industrial schedules but assured the farmers that the agricultural schedules would be raised to prevent the increasing importations of farm products.[7]

Not surprisingly, the proposed tariff hikes on manufactures were received favorably by investors. Sales and market share would increase, as would profits and earnings. This touched off a period of intense stock market speculation that lasted fourteen months (August 1928-September 1929). Adding fuel to the fire was the fact that New York governor Alfred E. Smith, the Democratic presidential candidate, was an unpopular figure and a long shot for the White House. Referring to the monthly Dow-Jones Industrial Average index data presented in Figures 4.4 and 4.5, we see that stock prices literally "took off" in August 1928, increasing nearly 11 percent (i.e. from 216.62 to 240.41).

From the official unveiling of Republican presidential hopeful Herbert Hoover's election platform to the November 6, 1928 election, the Dow Jones industrial Average index increased by more than 35 percent, going from an initial value of 216.62 to a value of 293.38. His victory by a margin of 407 to 69 sent stock prices soaring.

Figure 4.4
The Dow Jones Industrial Average, January 1928-December 1929

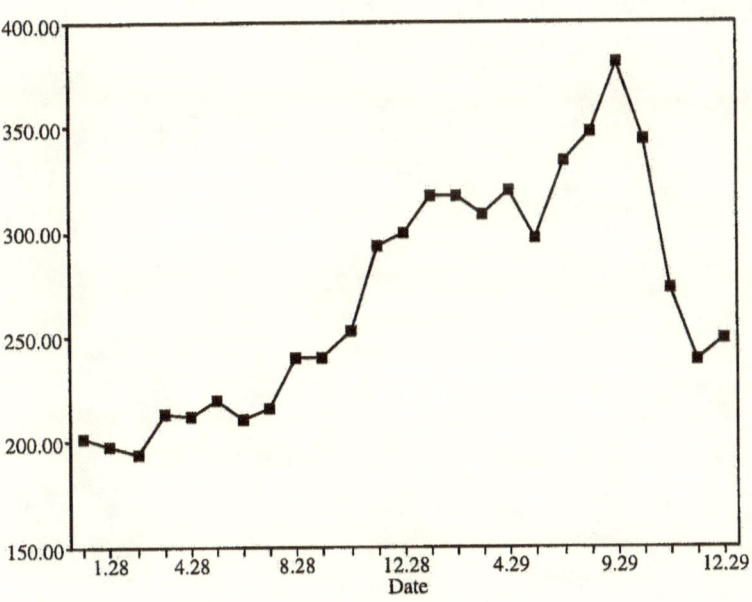

Source: Pierce (1991).

In the minds of investors, there was little doubt: the enactment of the proposed tariffs on manufactures was simply a matter of time. High external tariffs, by further shutting out imports, would increase sales, earnings, and profits, and close the gap between the nation's ability to produce and its ability to consume. The nation's EHTCFPT plants would run at capacity. The manufacturing lobby, which had been highly active at the Kansas City Republican convention, had triumphed.[8]

THE MANUFACTURING LOBBY

Calls for higher tariffs came primarily from the industrialized Northeast.[9] Leading the charge was Joseph A. Grundy, President of the *Pennsylvania Manufacturers Association* and a longtime Republican.[10] Grundy played an instrumental role in Hoover's victory at the *1928 Republican National Convention* in Kansas City. According to Harold U. Faulkner: "The Smoot-Hawley Tariff was an administrative measure put through the party machine and no single person was more active than Joseph R. Grundy, president of *The Pennsylvania Manufacturers Association*, who became Senator in December 1929" (1950, 342). His political agenda was limited to one item: a general upward tariff revision including manufactures.[11]

Figure 4.5
Stock Price Appreciation, January 1928-December 1929

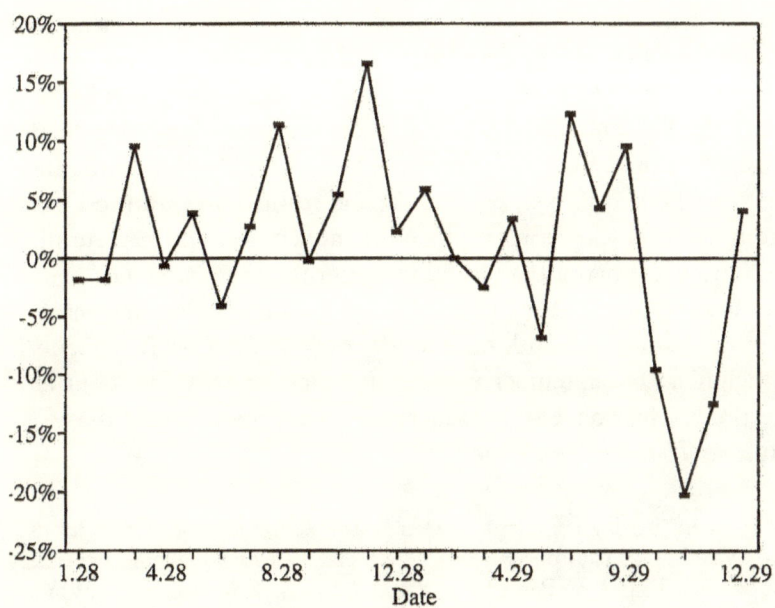

Source: Pierce (1991).

Unfortunately, there is no record of the rate hikes Grundy had in mind. Were tariffs on manufactures to rise by 10 percent, 20 percent, or 100 percent? What is known, however, is that when the Hawley Tariff Bill was put before the House in early 1928, Grundy was unhappy with the proposed rate revisions for manufactures. According to *The New York Times*:

> The dissatisfaction in highly protected industry because the bill does not increase rates on manufactured products is apparent from a statement of Joseph R. Grundy, president of the Pennsylvania Manufacturers' Association. Mr. Grundy had an interview with President Hoover not long ago, and while he would not comment on what took place behind the doors of the President's office, the impression was created that he had yielded to Mr. Hoover's desire that he should not insist on higher duties on industrial

products than the bill was then expected to provide. Today Mr. Grundy said: "The few rises that are in the bill fall short of meeting the requirements, which the past seven years of Pennsylvania's industries show, along the lines indicated in the Republican platform adopted at Kansas City."[12]

Whether he was satisfied with the final tariff revisions in the Hawley Tariff Bill is unknown. What is known, however, is that in the final stages of the debate over the Smoot-Hawley Tariff Bill in the Senate (i.e. in October 1929), Grundy supported the administration's tariff initiative. On October 29, 1929, with the Smoot-Hawley Tariff Bill was on what appeared to be its final leg, he called on the Senate to "silence the West," in reference to the Republican senators who had broken party ranks and teamed up with the Democrats with the intention of lowering tariffs on manufactures. One can surmise that Smoot-Hawley was better than nothing, better than the *status quo*.

Other leading protagonists—and Pennsylvanians—include Governor John S. Fisher and Samuel M. Vulcain, president of the *Baldwin Locomotive Works* of Philadelphia. On September 5, 1929, in a meeting with President Hoover, Fisher expressed his concerns over increasing pressure to amend the tariff bill. According to *The New York Times:*

> Earlier in the day President Hoover heard Representative Albert Johnson of Washington vigorously oppose the Senate Tariff bill, while two others, Governor Fisher of Pennsylvania and John E. Edgerton of New York, president of the National Manufactures Association, voiced protests against administrative features of the bill. Governor Fisher said that the American valuation plan was essential to a sound tariff bill and that protection could not be given to one group alone, but must be extended to the entire country. "During the campaign we preached protection for the East, West and all parts of the country," Governor Fisher said. "We in Pennsylvania are for a tariff that will afford protection for all of our industries. We expect agricultural protection, but we are not going to stand for recognition of any section to the disadvantage of another."[13]

In January 1928, Samuel M. Vulcain, addressing *The Chicago Association of Credit Men,* pointed out that high wages and high tariffs were essential for the preservation of prosperity in America.[14]

> Wages should not be governed solely by supply and demand, he asserted, but should be placed at a level which would enable workers to buy the necessities of life. It is the wage-earner who constitutes the great majority

of our population, he said. These people are the spenders of the nation and upon their ability to spend freely the general business of our country depends. Foreign importations should be avoided by all, he said. We may profit individually by buying foreign goods at less than American manufacturers can produce, but the injurious consequences to general business more than offset the selfish gain, he declares. A protective tariff is necessary if we are to have full dinner pails for our boys during 1928 and the years to come, he insisted.[15]

Coincidentally, at the turn of the century, Vulcain had described the Baldwin Locomotive Works favorable experience with the electric unit .

In conclusion, while the question of the saving in power which the adoption of electric motors permitted was of importance, it was by no means the deciding factor: I would have put electric driving systems not only if they saved no power, but even it they required several times the power of a shaft and belting system to operate. (Devine 1990, 31)

Samuel M. Vulcain's views personified U.S. industry in the 1910s and 1920s: increasingly productive (owing to EHTCFPT) and increasingly constrained on product markets. The electrification of U.S. industry had radically increased potential GNP; insufficient markets (income and demand), however, prevented it from realizing its potential.

TARIFFS AND PRICES

Opponents of the proposed tariff hikes argued that higher tariffs on manufactures would lead to higher prices. For example, U.S. farmers opposed the inclusion of manufactures on the grounds that the agricultural cost of living would rise. Manufacturers would respond by raising prices.

What is particularly interesting and, as it turns out, extremely revealing about the problem at hand is the fact that throughout the tariff debate, Senator Smoot repeatedly rejected this argument, insisting categorically that higher tariffs would not lead to higher prices. For example, *The New York Times* of September 13, 1929, reported that "Senator Smoot termed unjustified by facts the argument that increases in agricultural products were offset by those on industry. It was a fallacy, he said, to assume that the increased tariffs on manufactures would add to the costs of the farmer." Implicit in Senator Smoot's position is the assumption that EHTCFPT firms were on the non-increasing portion of their cost curves. Higher tariffs would secure a larger share of the domestic market for U.S. firms. Excess capacity, he reasoned, would guard against price hikes.

The battle lines had been drawn. Farmers opposed higher tariffs on imported manufactures on the grounds that they would raise prices. The Old-Guard Republicans disagreed, pointing to the presence of non-negligible excess capacity acting as a safeguard guard against higher prices. Separating the two was a debate that is as real today as it was in the 1920s, namely that over market clearing versus non market clearing. Opponents implicitly assumed that markets cleared, and that firms operated at economic capacity. In this case, tariff increases would push prices up as firms increased output beyond minimum average cost. Old-Guard Republicans and the nation's manufacturers disagreed; markets were not in equilibrium and, more importantly, firms were not operating at capacity.

Conclusion

As Yale University economics professor Irving Fisher argued in the fallout from the stock market crash in October 1929, the stock market boom of 1928-1929 was not the result of speculation. Anticipated earning and dividend growth in this period was tracking the nation's increased ability to produce, itself the result of a massive technology shock, namely, the electrification of U.S. industry. Fueling investor expectations was the Hoover administration's proposed tariff initiative. Higher tariffs on imports would push the U.S. economy on to the growth path defined by EHTCFPT's. Put differently, the policy instrument that had allowed the United States to go from mere colony to industrialized nation (see Chapter 1) would now enable it to realize its new found potential. As we shall see in the next chapter, this view was not shared by everyone. Farmers and foreign governments vigorously opposed the Smoot-Hawley Tariff Bill in its various incarnations. In the summer of 1929, a sure thing turned sour. Democrats and a group of thirteen Insurgent Republicans came out against the bill, arguing that tariffs would lead to higher prices and, invariable to retaliatory measures abroad. Now in control of the Senate, they steered the United States on to an altogether different course: tariffs on manufactures would fall. As we shall see, the stock market reacted in a predictable way: it factored the higher anticipated earnings and dividend growth out of stock prices—in short, it crashed.

5

The Fallout

The Republican tariff initiative, spearheaded by Old-Guard Republicans Senator Reed Smoot of Utah and Joseph R. Grundy, President of the Pennsylvania Manufacturers Association, attempted to close the gap between U.S. industry's increased ability to produce, and actual output. If all went according to plan, imports would decrease and production and sales of EHTCFPT U.S. firms would increase. Manufacturers welcomed the tariff bill: higher tariffs, they believed, would lead to higher sales, employment and earnings. Excess capacity would be put in service. Investors factored these anticipated, higher earnings into stock prices, believing that America's factories would soon produce at capacity.

However, the tide turned in the summer of 1929. America's trading partners denounced the proposed tariff bill, belligerently threatening to enact retaliatory tariff measures aimed at U.S. exports. More importantly, U.S. farmers reaffirmed their opposition to the bill on the grounds that the proposed tariffs on food imports, combined with the proposed tariffs on manufactures, would do nothing to improve their lot. The price of manufactures would increase, they reasoned, increasing their cost of living, thus negating any potential gain from higher tariffs on food imports. Opposition to the proposed tariff bill gained momentum in the summer and fall of 1929. In July 1929, thirteen Insurgent Republicans broke party rank and joined the Democrats in their attempt at defeating the proposed tariff bill. By October, the bill was "good-as-dead" in the minds of prominent Old-Guard Republicans. The stock market crashed when it became increasingly clear that the anticipated increases in sales, market share, and earnings would not materialize. In this chapter, a blow-by-blow account of the demise of the Smoot-Hawley Tariff Bill of 1929 and the ensuing stock market crash is provided.

On January 7, 1929, the House Committee on the Ways and Means began hearings on the proposed tariff bill. By February 27, 1929, the hearings had concluded. On April 15, Congress convened an extra session to deal with the tariff bill. On May 7, Willis C. Hawley of Oregon, chairman of the Ways and Means Committee, reported it to the House. On May 28, 1929, the House passed the bill (from which point it was known as the Hawley Tariff Bill). On June 13, the Senate Finance Committee, chaired by Senator Reed Smoot, began hearings on the bill.

Under the 1922 Fordney-McCumber Tariff Act, agricultural products benefited from an average rate of protection of 25.85 percent. Industrial products, on the other hand, benefited from an average rate of 42.03 percent The tariff bill passed in the House on May 28, 1929, raised the average rate of protection on agricultural products to 29.90 percent and the average rate of protection on industrial products to 47.07 percent Rates on industrial products would as such rise by 5 percent, while those on agricultural products would rise by 4 percent

This did not sit particularly well with the Democrats in the Senate. Higher prices on manufactures, they argued, would all but eliminate any gain that farmers could expect from higher tariffs on food products. In short, the Hawley Tariff Bill, which promised relief from shrinking markets and depressed prices would, on the whole, principally benefit the nation's manufacturers.[1] American farmers reacted. Their bottom line was tariff rate parity with industry. Leading the charge was Senator Walter F. George, Democrat from Georgia.

The average rate on industrial products in the Fordney-McCumber Tariff Act is 16.18 percent higher than the average agricultural rate; and in the bill as it is passed the House, industrial products have an average rate of 17.17 percent higher than agricultural products. The disparity between the two rates is thus widened between the two products. Whether the reaction from all parts of the country now making itself felt in Washington will bring about a reduction in the House rates remains to be seen. The farmer knows what he is getting in the tariff battle. If the majority party in the Senate refuses to take due notice of the rising tide of opposition to the House rates, the farmer, along with all consumers, may expect a boost in living costs.[2]

Opposition to the Hawley Tariff Bill was not confined to rural America. France reacted swiftly calling for the creation of a "united front" against the United States. Gathering in Amsterdam on July 7, 1929, Europe's delegates to the *Assembly of World Business* denounced the Hawley Tariff Bill vehemently. As *The New York Times* reported on July 8, 1929, France and other European nations stood united in their determination "to counter-attack."

> The fifth biennial congress of the International Chamber of Commerce opens here tomorrow morning with the proposed upward revision of the American tariff as the dominant if unofficial issue. The agenda, in its long list of world trade problems, does not mention this provocative question, but most of the 1,200 delegates now assembling in Amsterdam from more than forty countries have made it quite clear that the American tariff is uppermost in their minds.[3]

France called for the creation of international committees, one for each branch of industry doing business with the United States. According to *The New York Times*, these groups "would study how best to supplant American exports to Europe, either of domestic production or from purchases from other European countries."[4] The committees would also study the question of finding markets to replace the American market. Clearly, opposition to the proposed tariff was mounting.

By this point in time, the Hoover administration's much-anticipated tariff initiative was in trouble. Opposition, both domestic and international, was on the rise. Sensing the approaching storm, on July 18, 1929, the Senate Finance Committee suspended hearings. On July 22, Republican members of the committee, determined to achieve passage, began rewriting the Bill with an ear to the farmers' demand for equity. The following day, however, the roof literally caved in: thirteen Republican Senators, led by Republican Senator William A. Borah of Idaho, announced that they had broken party rank and would work with the Democrats to defeat the Smoot-Hawley Tariff Bill. *The New York Times* reported this sudden unexpected turn of events as follows:

> Just as the Republicans of the Senate Finance Committee completed consideration of the tariff bill this afternoon, Senator Borah of Idaho denounced the measure as a violation of Republican pledges to agriculture and demanded its defeat. Another Progressive Republican, Senator Brookhart of Iowa and Senator McKellar, Democrat of Tennessee, charged that the Finance Committee Republicans had failed to put the farmer on a

basis equal with industry. They, like Mr. Borah, asserted that the Republican Committee men had not improved the bill as compared with the House measure so far as the farmer was concerned. In his denunciation of the bill, Senator Borah asserted that there would never have been any special session of Congress nor any tariff revision had the purpose not been to relieve agriculture. But now, he added, if either the House or the Senate tariff bills were passed, the farmer would continue to suffer the same inequity with industry that he was under today.[5]

What led these Insurgent Republicans to oppose the Tariff Bill? Was it the expected political fallout in the 1930 Congressional elections? Was it a matter of principle? Was it fear of a full-scale tariff war with France and England? While the reasons are, to this day, unclear, what was clear was the fact that the chances that the Smoot-Hawley Tariff Bill would pass before October were dwindling rapidly.

Not helping matters was President Herbert C. Hoover's apparent indifference to the tariff bill. While the promise of "tariffs, tariffs and more tariffs" had swept him into office in November 1928, he apparently soured on the idea of further increasing tariffs on manufactures. Throughout much of the tariff debate in both the House and the Senate, he remained silent.[6]

THE STOCK MARKET CRASHES

Holding the balance of power in the Senate, the Insurgent Republican-Democratic coalition drafted its own tariff plank: maintain or raise tariffs on food products and lower tariffs on manufactures. Higher tariffs were needed to stimulate agriculture. However, manufacturing was in need of no such stimulation. Many argued correctly that the trade balance in manufactures was improving annually. So effective was the coalition in its opposition to the tariff bill that on September 6, 1929, a disgruntled Senator Smoot informed President Hoover that the date of passage of the proposed legislation was "now uncertain."[7] The stumbling block was the very scope of the proposed tariff initiative. The administration favored the inclusion of all goods, including manufactures, while the Democrats and Insurgent Republicans pushed for lower rates on manufactures.[8] The stage was therefore set: Senator Smoot and other Old-Guard Republicans favored an across-the-board tariff hike, while Democratic Senator Furnifold M. Simmons and Republican Senator William E. Borah favored a limited tariff bill.

Visibly nervous about the pending tariff bill, the nation's manufacturers urged the Senate to "speed up tariff legislation." Holding its 34th annual convention at the Roosevelt Hotel in New York, the *National Association of Manufacturers* (NAM) reaffirmed its support for higher tariffs. The tariff bill was the chief topic of discussion. H.L. Derby, president of the Kalbfleisch Corporation and chairman of the NAM's tariff committee, pointed out that the tariff struggle of the past year (i.e. 1929) had "created unrest; slowed up business, and resulted is delaying and some cases, abandoning new projects."[9] A resolution "urging Congress to speed up pending legislation" was adopted. According to *The New York Times:* "The resolution on the tariff reflected the views of the speakers. Pointing out that business "can be seriously injured," by uncertainty over tariff schedules and declaring the necessity for flexible provisions permitting the adjustment of our tariff rates to changing economic conditions and shifts in foreign policy."[10]

The outcome weighed heavily on the minds of investors. If the Democratic-Insurgent Republican coalition succeeded in either killing or watering down the Smoot-Hawley Tariff Bill, then the anticipated increases in market shares, profits, and earnings would not materialize. The market downturns of October 23-24, 1929 and October 29, 1929 were the direct result of two pieces of tariff-based "bad news."[11] The first occurred on October 21, 1929 when the Senate defeated the *Thomas Recommittal Plan* to limit tariff revisions to the duties on farm products. According to *The New York Times:*

> By the overwhelming vote of 64 to 10, the Senate this afternoon refused to adopt the motion of Senator Thomas, Democrat of Oklahoma, to limit tariff revision to the duties on farm products. Only a handful of the members of the Democratic-Progressive coalition supported the Thomas motion. Just before the vote, Senator Simmons, ranking minority member of the Finance Committee, revealed that Democrats at least want the rates on industrial articles kept before the Senate because they wish to reduce not only the duties recommended by the committee, but those in the existing Fordney-McCumber law.[12]

The roof had literally caved in: tariff rates on manufactures would, in all likelihood, fall. The second piece of "bad news" occurred on Wednesday, October 22, 1929. Emboldened by its victory on the 21st, the Democratic-Insurgent Republican coalition went on the offensive, taking aim at existing tariff rates on manufactures. Their first target was the tariff on medicinal tannic acid. Senator Alben W. Barkley, Democrat from Kentucky, moved to cut the duty to 18 cents a pound from the 20 cent rate proposed by the Senate Finance Committee and the House-proposed rate of 22 cents. The motion passed by a margin of 12 votes, with 45 Senators voting for and 33 against. As it turned out, this seemingly innocuous event changed the course of U.S. and world economic history. Its importance cannot be overstated. It marked a radical shift in U.S. tariff policy: rates on manufactures would be reduced; rates on farm products would either increase or remain unchanged. As *The New York Times* described it: "The item on which the vote was taken was incidental, but the result signaled that the coalition was nearly intact in its initial drive and also that it still held control in the Senate."[13] The stock market reacted swiftly and predictably, losing 27 points on the following two days.[14]

While this was not the first piece of tariff-related "bad news," it was by far the most damning. Up until Senator Barkley's motion, it was generally felt that the opposition to the Smoot-Hawley Tariff Bill would somehow be dealt with, presumedly by increasing rates on agricultural products. Wall Street remained confident that an agreement would be reached. For example, stock prices fell only slightly after the thirteen Insurgent Republicans broke party ranks on July 22, 1929. It is important to note that from this point on, the Democratic-Insurgent Republican coalition sought to change the tariff bill, not to defeat it. Clearly, Wall Street understood this.

In hindsight, one cannot overstate the fallout from Senator Barkley's motion. Old-Guard Republican Senators, feeling outnumbered and out maneuvered, were now prepared to abandon the proposed tariff bill as evidenced by Republican Senator David E. Reed's Philadelphia address on October 27, 1929 in which he predicted that the Tariff Bill would die in the "present session."[15] Clearly, existing tariff rates on manufactures (i.e. those contained in the Fordney-McCumber Tariff Act) were preferred to the lower tariffs proposed by the Democratic-Insurgent Republican coalition. The ensuing rebuttal by Senators Smoot and Borah, and statements by Senator Simmons to the effect that "the Democratic party intended to see to it that the President's plan to relieve agriculture was carried out," sealed the fate of the tariff bill in investors' minds." The hoped-for higher tariffs on manufactures would not materialize, a realization that sent stock prices spiraling downwards for a second time.[16] America's factories would not operate at full capacity. In fact, capacity utilization would fall as tariff rates on manufactures came down. Referring to Figures 4.4 and 4.5 in Chapter 4, we see that in October the *Dow Jones Industrial Average* fell eight percent, and in November, it fell another 28 percent, to 250.

By December, the *Dow Jones Industrial Average* had returned to its pre-Hoover tariff initiative level (i.e. July 1928). The stock market crashes had simply factored the anticipated tariff-induced earnings out of stock prices. The much-anticipated increased sales, profits, and earnings would simply not materialize.

FUNDAMENTALS RESUSCITATED

The stock market boom of 1928-1929 was not a speculative bubble (Shiller 1981; Barsky and De Long 1990; White 1990). Stock-price movements throughout this period were predicated on changing fundamentals. The electrification of U.S. industry increased greatly productivity and productive capacity. The Smoot-Hawley Tariff Bill of 1929 provided investors with the hope of realizing this potential, of higher profits and earnings. By October 1929, it was clear, however, that the Hoover administration's tariff initiative was doomed. The stock market reacted rationally, factoring out tariff bill-based gains.

That the Smoot-Hawley Tariff Bill did not pass in the Senate in the fall of 1929 as had been anticipated raises a number of counterfactual questions. For example, what if the thirteen Insurgent Republicans had not broken party ranks? What if President Hoover had campaigned in favor of the tariff bill? Would stock prices nonetheless have collapsed?

Clearly, we have no way of knowing. What we do know, however, is that given the underlying cause of the stock market boom and the reactions of America's trading partners, the crash was inevitable. The Smoot-Hawley Tariff Bill, being based on import substitution, could not succeed. In the short run, the U.S. manufacturers' market share may have increased at the expense of say British and French market share; however, in the long run, retaliatory tariffs on U.S. exports abroad would have cut short any gain and undoubtedly contributed to lower stock prices. History bears this out. Following the enactment of the Smoot-Hawley Tariff Bill in June of 1930, France, Germany and Canada responded with retaliatory tariff legislation aimed specifically at the United States. In 1931, Britain imposed duties on imports of manufactures.

IRVING FISHER ON THE STOCK MARKET CRASH

The stock market boom was not a speculative bubble. Higher expected earnings, based on America's increased capacity to produce combined with the almost certain passage of the Smoot-Hawley Tariff Bill, and not pure speculation, fueled this vertiginous rise in stock prices. Yale University economics professor Irving Fisher made a similar argument. On the day after the first crash (i.e. October 24, 1929), he declared that:

> The stock market rose after the war above the pre-war level by 50-100 percent because of war inflation, and that since, it has doubled because of increasing prosperity from less unstable money, new mergers, new scientific management, and the new labor policy of waste saving.[17]

One year later, in a book entitled *The Stock Market Crash and After*, he was more explicit:

> But after 1919, something happened. The implications of which are not yet sufficiently gauged. It was of enough significance to cause President Hoover's Committee on Recent Economic Changes to remark that "acceleration rather than structural change is the key to an understanding of our recent economic developments." The committee added: "But the breadth and the tempo of recent developments gives them new importance." What happened was indicated by the fact that in the United States, eight million, three hundred thousand workers produced in 1925 one quarter more than nine million wage workers turned out in 1919. The new indexes of the Federal Reserve Board measuring production record this gratifying advance which reflects an increase in the American standard of living. The indexes cover, directly and indirectly, four-fifths of the industrial productivity of the nation directly in about thirty-five industries, and collaterally, in many more. The general volume of production had increased between 1919 and 1927 by 46.5 percent; primary power by 22 percent; and primary power per wage earner by 30.9 percent (between 1919 and 1925) and productivity per wage worker by 53.5 percent between 1919 and 1927. (Fisher 1930, 120)

Among the causes of this phenomenal increase in productivity, he argued, was the electrification of U.S. industry: Fisher was convinced that electric power lay at the root of the stock market crash. Among these is what Fisher refers to in his book as "Fear About the Tariff."

> Many will take seriously Mr. Kent's further contention that the market fell because of fear engendered in the public mind by the action of the coalition bloc in Congress in connection with the tariff bill. In the panicky condition of the market everything added to its fears. But big business had no reason to fear any fall of the tariff and little fear if it were not raised. Representatives of the automobile industry, the country's largest industry, told the

President that they wished lower tariff protection for their products, some of them even saying that absolute removal of the tariff would not hurt them. No doubt business was disturbed by failure to decide the tariff question, quite irrespective of its merits. It might be argued that fears of a higher and of a lower tariff hurt business. In any case the tariff is today not a small element in the calculations of the business of the country generally. Mr. Kent is not a lone voice crying in the speculative wilderness when he says "As soon as dealers in securities who were constantly on the watch for indications as to business changes, realized that this feeling of uneasiness [on account of the tariff bill] was spreading throughout industry, they began selling stocks." But it was the dilatoriness of the Senate, not the need of a higher tariff, that hurt business. (Fisher 1930, 48)

Unfortunately, Fisher had not grasped the role played by the tariff bill in the stock market boom. Nowhere does he mention overproduction and/or oversupply. Nor does he as much refer to the motives underlying the original tariff bill (i.e. those expressed by Republican Senator Reed Smoot). Nowhere is this more evident than in the petition sent by Fisher and 1,027 other economists in May 1930 to President Herbert C. Hoover asking him to veto the tariff bill. Nowhere is the growing weakness of the U.S. economy (employment and output) in the months and years preceding the stock market crash, mentioned by Senators Wagner and Smoot in the Senate in March 1928 mentioned. Clearly, while Fisher appreciated the role played by electric power in altering economic and financial fundamentals, he failed to appreciate the role of the Smoot-Hawley Tariff Bill in the stock market crash.

FINAL PASSAGE: THE SMOOT-HAWLEY TARIFF ACT OF 1930

Like a phoenix rising from its ashes, the Smoot-Hawley Tariff Bill, left for dead by Old-Guard Republicans in October 1929, went on to live an illustrious life, earning the title of the most restrictive tariff law ever framed in the history of the Western civilization. How did this happen? After all, by December 1929, the bill was "as good as dead?" Old-Guard Republicans, led by Senator Smoot, favored both manufactures and agricultural products. Democrats, however, favored a limited tariff bill. Manufactures, they argued, ought to be excluded. As the trade figures presented in Chapter 4 showed, their reasoning was factually sound: manufactures had not been unduly hurt by imports.

Despite being a Republican initiative, thirteen Republican Senators opposed the bill which had passed the House (i.e. the Hawley Tariff Bill). Together with the Democrats, they successfully blocked its passage in the fall of 1929. The Insurgent Republican-Democratic coalition was also instrumental in defeating the *Thomas Amendment*, which called for a limited tariff bill (i.e. involving farm products only), and which, as pointed out, eventually led to the stock market crashes of October 1929.

Locked in a war of wills, Insurgent Republicans and Democrats on one side, and Old-Guard Republicans on the other, remained deadlocked throughout November and December; the former were not willing to either accept or increase existing tariff levels on manufactures, and the latter were not willing to exclude them. The tide, however, turned in late December. Visibly unhappy about the turn of events, on December 22, 1929, the nation's farmers, some two million strong, forwarded what *The New York Times* referred to as an "address to Congress," urging it to enact a tariff law that "places agriculture on a parity with industry." *The New York Times* reported:

> Tariff legislation is developing a bitter factional contest within the Republican party, with the appearance today of an aggressive opposition among 2,000,000 farmers who promise to make their influence felt in the 1930 primaries and election unless they obtain a tariff bill satisfactory to the agrarian West. These 2,000,000 farmers, just as Congress has adjourned, have forwarded an address to the Senate objecting to the views of the editors of newspapers in the Northwest who counseled expedition in the passage of a tariff bill with the industrial rates of the present law unchanged.[18]

Being the wily politician he was, Senator Smoot seized this once in-a-lifetime opportunity. With the threat of defeat looming over the thirteen Insurgent Republicans, Smoot upped the *ante* by raising the proposed tariff in the Smoot-Hawley Tariff Bill on imported sugar.[19] The Democratic-Insurgent Republican coalition floundered, and in six months, the Smoot-Hawley Tariff Bill as amended in the summer of 1929 was signed into law (June 17, 1930).[20]

THE STOCK-MARKET CRASH AND THE GREAT DEPRESSION

At the root of the stock market boom and crash of 1928-1929 was the electrification of U.S. industry and the resulting extremely-high-throughput, continuous-flow production techniques. The sequence of events from electrification to the crash is as follows: The electrification of U.S. industry in the 1910s and 1920s resulted in higher productivity, greater productive capacity, and, owing to the problem of underincome, greater unemployment, which, in turn, prompted Senator Reed Smoot and other Old-Guard Republicans to seek policy measures aimed at increasing capacity utilization and employment. Not understanding why the U.S. economy failed to produce at capacity, they resorted to an old Republican party policy instrument workhorse, namely higher tariffs. Smoot, the chairman of the Senate Finance Committee, made tariffs the key issue at the 1928 party convention. Herbert C. Hoover, the heir apparent to outgoing president, Calvin Coolidge, campaigned on a platform of higher tariffs for manufacturers and farmers, and lower taxes. Hoover's victory at the Kansas City Republican convention, and, subsequently, in the November 1928 presidential election, sent stock prices spiraling upward as investors factored in anticipated higher sales, market share, and earnings.

Over the course of the ensuing seven months (November 1928 to July 1929), Wall Street broke record after record. For years, businessmen and investors knew that productivity and productive capacity had increased markedly. Now, something was being done to realize this potential. Tariffs on foreign manufactures would increase. Things soured, however, in July 1929 when thirteen Insurgent Republicans broke party ranks and announced they would work with the Democrats to defeat the proposed tariff bill. The showdown occurred in October 1929, when the Insurgent Republican-Democratic coalition called for lower, not higher tariffs on manufactures. Wall Street reacted immediately: the stock market crashed. America would not realize its new found potential.

THE GREAT DEPRESSION

The stock market crash of October 1929 sent the U.S. economy spiraling into the deepest depression in its history. Investment activity virtually dried up, setting off a complex chain of events that culminated in the worst industrial crisis in U.S. history. This section presents an alternative explanation of the Great Depression. Specifically, the Great Depression was the product of two major developments. The first was the electrification of U.S. industry from 1910 to 1929. Electric power revolutionized U.S. industry, radically increasing its capacity to produce. The second was tariff bill-related excess productive capacity. The Republican tariff initiative generated record levels of investment in 1928 and 1929 as firms that either had not *Fordized*, or that had and were operating at capacity, invested in anticipation of the passage of the tariff bill. Together, these generated significant excess capacity.

As mentioned, the demise of the Smoot-Hawley Tariff Bill in October 1929 came as a shock to investors. The defeat of the *Thomas Recommittal Plan* made it clear that domestic firms' market share would not increase at the expense of their foreign rivals. Not surprisingly, investment expenditure plummeted, further widening the gap between potential and actual U.S. GNP. As investment expenditure fell, consumption expenditure followed suit. In time, the gap widened. Making matters worse was the continued surge in productivity in the early 1930s. Paradoxically, from 1929 to 1932, productivity increased in the U.S. economy. Referring to Figure 2.1, we see that electric power consumption per employee in manufacturing increased 21 percent over the course of this period, rising from 5,150 to 6,276 kilowatt hours per annum.[21] Clearly, the diffusion of EHTCFPT's continued unfettered during the Great Depression.[22]

Figure 5.1
U.S. Investment Expenditure—Manufacturing, 1920-1930

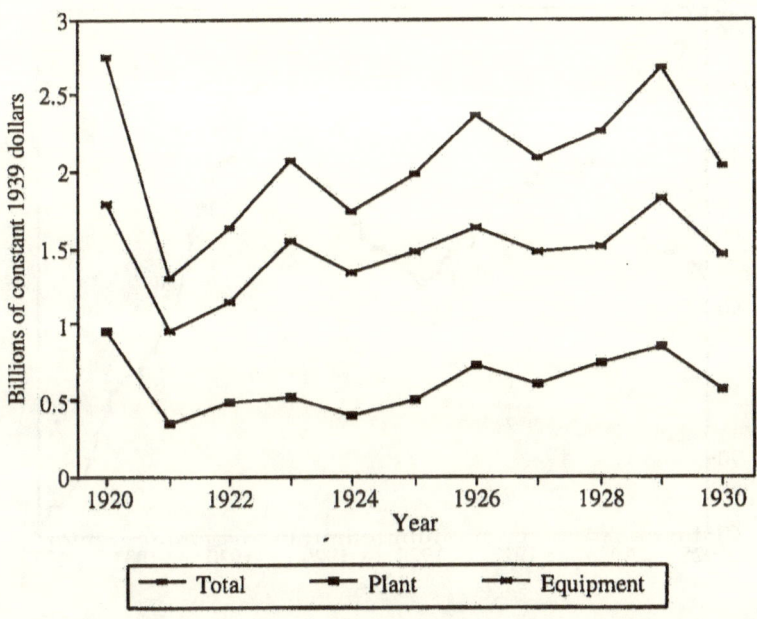

Source: The National Industrial Conference Board (1943), 243.

What was the extent of excess capacity in the 1920s? Edwin G. Nourse and five associates at the Brooking Institution, including Harold Moulton, provided numerical estimates of excess capacity in U.S. industry in the 1920s. Data on operating capacity and output were collected by surveying manufacturers. Their results showed that in 1929, U.S. industry was operating at 84 to 86 percent of capacity.

TARIFF BILL-INDUCED INVESTMENT

The Smoot-Hawley Tariff Bill was both a cause and an effect of excess capacity. Electrification resulted in significant excess capacity in U.S. industry. However, not all firms adopted EHTCFPT's. The Smoot-Hawley Tariff Bill, with its higher sales and market share, prompted laggard firms to *Fordize*, further widening the gap between potential and actual GNP.

Figure 5.2
U.S. Factory Employment-Machinery, January 1926-December 1931

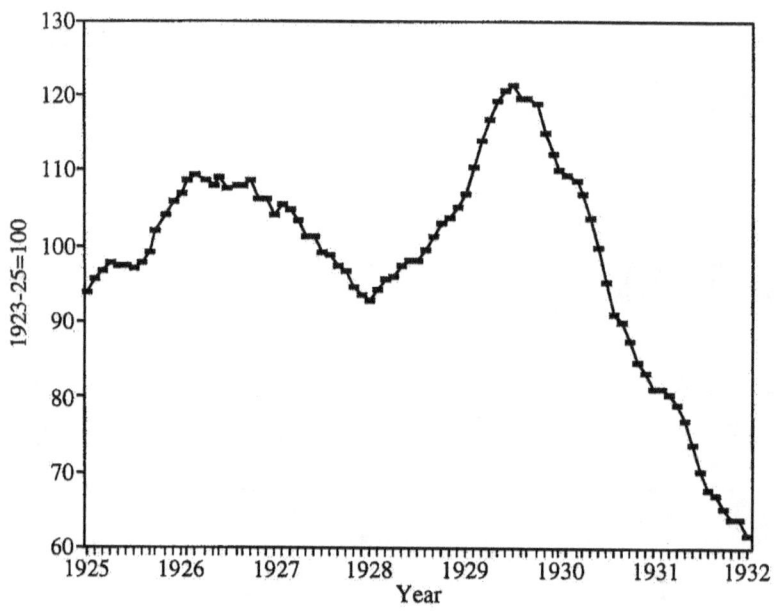

Source: U.S. Department of Commerce (1932).

Referring to Figure 5.1, total investment expenditure in U.S. manufacturing peaked in 1929 at $2.683 billion (constant 1939 dollars). 1928 and 1929 were as such banner years as far as investment is concerned. To what extent was the proposed Smoot-Hawley Tariff Bill responsible for this increase? To answer this question, consider monthly data. Since data on manufacturing investment *per se* are not available, investment expenditure was proxied using employment in the machinery industry as defined by the *Survey of Current Business*. The data presented in Figure 5.2 show that employment in this sector increased at a record pace from July 1928 to July 1929, the heyday of the Smoot-Hawley Tariff Bill. Also of interest is the extent to which employment in this sector of the U.S. economy tracks stock prices (see Figure 3.4 in Chapter 3). Specifically, the relevant index (1923-1925=100) went from 97.9 in July 1928 to 121.5 in July 1929. Anticipated higher sales, earnings, and profits from the Hoover administration's tariff initiative pushed up the value of the nation's capital stock as well as the capital stock itself.

As mentioned, a week before the stock market crash, the *National Association of Manufacturers* (NAM), meeting in New York City, urged the government to speed up the pending "tariff legislation." H. L. Derby, president of the Kalbfleisch Corporation and chairman of the NAM's tariff committee, pointed out that the delay in adopting the Smoot-Hawley Tariff Bill was responsible for a decrease in investment. According to the *New York Times:* "The tariff struggle of the past year (i.e. 1929) has created unrest, slowed up business, and resulted in delaying and in some cases, abandoning new projects."[23] A resolution "urging Congress to speed up pending legislation" was adopted.

The Great Depression was the product of two opposing forces: rising productivity and falling demand, particularly investment demand. Productive capacity had increased dramatically throughout the 1920s, buoyed by (a) the on-going electrification of U.S. industry (see Figure 2.4) and (b) the Republican administration's tariff bill. The failure of the latter sent stock prices crashing, bringing planned investment expenditure to a halt, which in turn set off a complex chain of events known as the Great Depression (see Figure 5.3). On Sunday, October 20, 1929, just days before the first stock market crash, Senator Watson of Indiana pointed to the tariff as being "vital to stable business." According to *The New York Times:*

Figure 5.3
U.S. Macroeconomic Aggregates 1929-1939

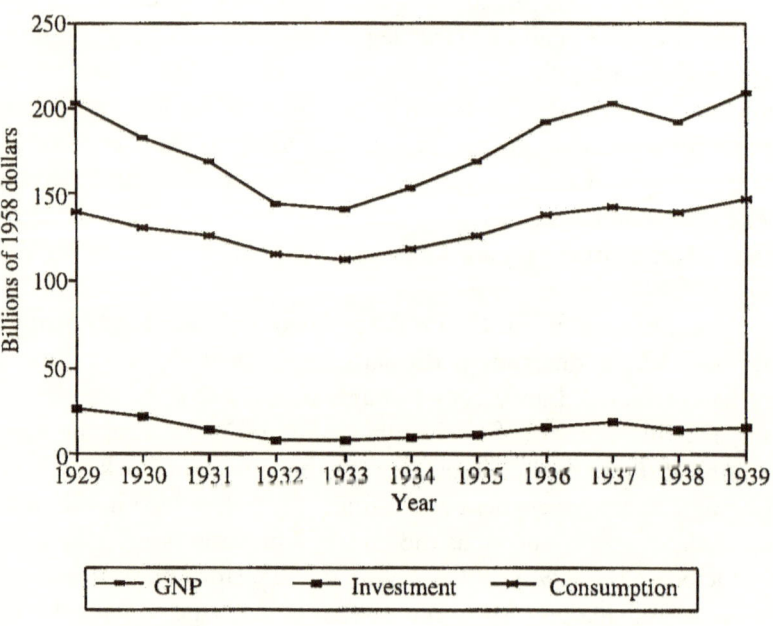

Source: U.S. Department of Commerce (1975), series F47, F48, F56.

Declaring that delay in the enactment of a tariff bill was slowing down business and injuring prosperity, Senator Watson of Indiana, Republican leader of the Senate, pleaded today for expedition in the Chamber and urged all forces to consider the pending bill with fairness and a national outlook, to the end that the West and East would obtain adequate protection and business might continue its onward progress. He said that the business man was hesitating to make heavy commitments until economic conditions were stabilized by a new tariff law. He saw in the New York stock market break at the end of the week one reaction that might be charged to Senate inability to hasten the passage of the bill.[24]

This is illustrated in Figure 5.4, where electric power consumption per employee, National Bureau of Economic Research-defined labor productivity, and investment are plotted from 1929 to 1939. Electric power consumption per worker increased 22 percent from 1929 to 1933. Labor productivity increased 18 percent from 1929 to 1936. Investment expenditure, however, decreased monotonically from 1929 to 1933; by 1933, it had fallen 71 percent.

Figure 5.4
U.S. Macroeconomic Indexes, 1929-1939

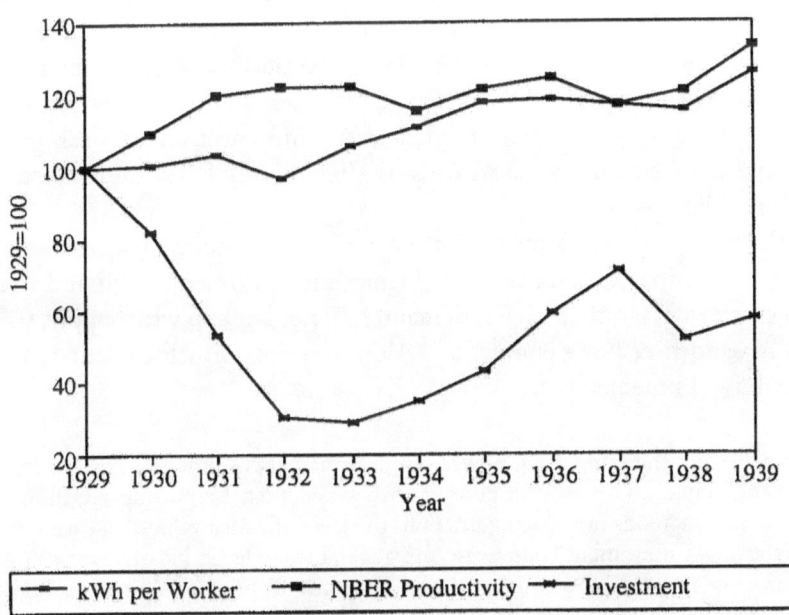

Source: U.S. Department of Commerce (1975), series D685, F56.

The severity and duration of the Great Depression, we argue, were directly proportional to the magnitude of the technology shock. The electrification of U.S. industry in conjunction with the capital investment induced by the Smoot-Hawley Tariff Bill contributed to increasing America's ability to produce (create wealth). Throughout the late 1920s and all of the 1930s, the U.S. economy was characterized by generalized excess capacity. Before investment expenditure could once again reach its pre-crash level, existing capacity would have to be fully utilized.

HENRY FORD AND EDWARD A. FILENE'S DIAGNOSES

Did Henry Ford and/or Edward. A. Filene foresee the Great Depression? A careful reading of their writings shows that neither predicted/foresaw a depression as severe as that which hit the U.S. economy in 1929. While both referred to the growing gap between productive capacity and output, neither appears to appreciate the role played by the Hoover administration's ill-fated tariff initiative. In a 1926 interview with Samuel Crowther, Henry Ford pointed out that "the way to check a threatened business depression is to cut prices and increase wages." He explained: "It is good business always to raise wages and never to lower them. Higher wages and lower prices mean greater power and more customers."[25] As early as 1926, Henry Ford, the analyst, had sensed trouble.

Unshaken by the developments in the early 1930s and the widespread calls for wage reductions as a means of reducing unemployment, Ford and Filene remained steadfast in their views: demand had not kept up with supply; wages would have to rise. For example, at a 1929 meeting with President Hoover, Ford pointed to the need of:

> increasing the purchasing power of our principal customers—The American People...This can be done in two ways: first, by putting additional value into goods or reducing prices to the level of actual values; and second, starting a movement to increase the general wage level. Nearly everything in this country is too high priced. The only thing that should be high priced in this country is the man who works. Wages must not come down, they must not even stay at their present level; they must go up. (Fisher 1930, 25)

In 1933, throwing his support behind the National Industrial Recovery Act of 1933 (NIRA), Ford declared:

> We've got to stop that gouging process if we want to see all of the people reasonably prosperous. There is only one rule for industrialists and that is: Make the best quality of goods possible at the lowest cost paying the highest wages possible. Nothing can be right in this country until wages are right. The life of business comes forth from the people in orders. The factories are not stopped for lack of money but for lack of orders. Money loaned at the top means nothing. Money spent at the bottom starts everything. I think that if industrial leaders had been willing to push wages up and up during the last thirty years the present economic ills would at least

not be as great as they are. If the government can help in these matters, well and good, but the government has not a rosy record in running itself thus far.

Like Ford, Edward A. Filene remained equally steadfast in his beliefs. Higher wages and shorter hours were required. In a speech to the Harvard Club on June 11, 1930, less than a week before the final passage of the Smoot-Hawley Tariff Act, he criticized the Hoover administration's push for higher tariffs, arguing instead for mass distribution:

> The interests of this country are best served by a fair trading basis between us and Europe and a high tariff would surely prove detrimental.... A moderate tariff on certain products may be advisable. But a high prohibitive tariff will make it impossible for us to sell goods abroad in large quantities and will endanger seriously our economic structure.... Mass production is the secret of prosperity.... Mass production...depends on mass distribution. We can't have one without the other in America or Europe or anywhere else.[26]

Throughout the Great Depression, Ford and Filene steadfastly continued their campaign for higher wages, shorter hours, and lower prices, earning the wrath of the business community in general. To the average businessman, raising wages when sales and revenues were falling made absolutely no sense—if anything, wages should fall, or so they thought (*Propositions 1* and *2*).

Conclusion

Alan Meltzer (1976) argued that the Smoot-Hawley Tariff Act converted what at the time was a sizeable recession into a severe depression. That is, the breakdown of U.S. and world trade transformed what was a "sizeable recession" into a "severe depression." Our results point to an alternative sequence of events, and to an alternative role for the Smoot-Hawley tariff Act. Specifically, the Smoot-Hawley Tariff Act did not cause the Great Depression; rather, against a backdrop of underincome, excess capacity, and weakening factor markets, it raised expectations, stimulated investment expenditure, and, in the end, prompted a precipitous decline in investment, sending the economy spiralling downwards, the end result of which was the Great Depression. Its severity, We argue, had less to do with the breakdown of world trade (owing to Smoot-Hawley) than it did to the chasm that separated the U.S. economy's new-found potential, and its failure to realize it.

6

The Second Policy Response: The National Industrial Recovery Act of 1933

Higher tariffs on imported manufactures, Senator Reed Smoot of Utah reasoned, would increase output and employment. America would prosper at the expense of its trading partners. Domestic and foreign opposition, however, postponed final approval of the Republican party's blueprint for a prosperous America. The fallout was catastrophic: the stock market crashed, bringing with it private investment, the end result of which was the Great Depression. The Smoot-Hawley Tariff Bill, signed into law on June 17, 1930, led to retaliatory tariffs on the part of its trading partners aimed at U.S. exports.

By the fall of 1930, it was painfully clear that import substitution-based growth could not and would not solve the problem that continued to plague the U.S. economy, namely generalized excess capacity. Put simply, America could not export its problem. Income, and specifically wage income, would have to rise, reasoned Democratic Senator Robert F. Wagner. This section examines the second policy response to oversupply, namely the National Industrial Recovery Act of 1933 (NIRA) which sought to increase income, specifically wage income, as a means of addressing the problem of oversupply/excess capacity. The National Industrial Recovery Act of 1933 called for a wholesale change to wage—and price-setting behavior in U.S. industry. The federal government would coordinate the process of wage and price determination.

It will be argued, however, that while the architects and main proponents of the NIRA had correctly diagnosed the problem plaguing the U.S. economy in the 1920s as the failure of expenditure to increase commensurately with productive capacity, they misdiagnosed the reasons for this failure. Senator Wagner, its chief proponent, pointed to higher profits as the cause. Overall income had increased in response to technological change; however, the owners of capital had appropriated the increase in its entirety. The data, we show, do not support this view. Profit income as a proportion of total income did not increase in the 1920s. Instead, the problem was underincome: aggregate U.S. income had not increased commensurately with U.S. productive capacity.

Enter Franklin D. Roosevelt

From October 1929 to November 1932, the U.S. economy slid into the worst industrial depression of its history. Real GNP fell 30 percent, from $203.6 billion (constant 1958 dollars) to $144.2 billion in 1932 (see Figure 5.3 in Chapter 5). Despite a series of measures aimed at stemming the tide, conditions continued to worsen. The 1932 presidential election brought New York governor Franklin D. Roosevelt to power. Within six months of assuming office, Roosevelt signed into law The National Industrial Recovery Act, the first a series of government policies aimed at restoring full employment. The National Industrial Recovery Act, like the Smoot-Hawley Tariff Bill, sought to correct the imbalance between aggregate supply and aggregate demand. To this end, measures would be taken to increase real wages throughout the economy, reduce working hours, and eliminate unethical employment practices. In short, competition would be replaced by cooperation. Firms would cooperatively set wages and prices at the industry level, and new government institutions would be created to oversee the workings of this radical transformation of industrial behavior. Logistically, the challenge was immense: detailed data on productivity, wages, costs, and prices by industry and/or product would be required.

THE NATIONAL INDUSTRIAL RECOVERY ACT OF 1933

The National Industrial Recovery Act of 1933 consisted of three titles, "Industrial Recovery," "Public Works and Construction Projects," "Amendments to Emergency Relief and Construction Act and Miscellaneous Provisions." In this chapter, the focus is on the first title, "Industrial Recovery," which outlines the proposed transformation of U.S. industry in ten sections (see Appendix B). Sections 1 and 2 describe the purpose and scope of the legislation. Section 1 declared the following:

> A national emergency productive of widespread unemployment and disorganization of industry, which burdens interstate and foreign commerce, affects the public welfare, and undermines the standards of living of the American people is hereby declared to exist. It is hereby declared to be the policy of congress to remove obstructions to the free flow of interstate and foreign commerce which tend to diminish the amount thereof; and to provide for the general welfare by promoting the organization of industry for the purpose of cooperative action among trade groups, to induce and maintain united action of labor and management under adequate governmental sanctions and supervision, to eliminate unfair competitive practices, to promote the fullest possible utilization of the present productive capacity of industries, to avoid undue restriction of production (except as may be temporarily required), to increase the consumption of industrial and agricultural products by increasing purchasing power, to reduce and relieve unemployment, to improve standards of labor, and otherwise rehabilitate industry and to conserve natural resources.[1]

Section 2 authorized the president to establish agencies to carry out this radical transformation of industry. Sections 3 through 7 described the workings of the "new" economy. Section 3, entitled "Codes of Fair Competition" was the *de facto* cornerstone of the act. It single-handedly redefined firm behavior in U.S. industry. Under the watchful eye of the National Recovery Administration (NRA), the government agency set up to administer the act, firms would meet to set wages, prices, and hours. Approval was not automatic as a number of conditions, set out in Section 3, would have to be met. Violations would be dealt with under the *Federal Trade Commission Act*. In short, unbridled competition would be replaced with "fair competition," based on interfirm communication and coordination.

The NIRA set out to alter radically the workings of the U.S. economy. Competition, the cornerstone of U.S. economic, political and social policy, would be replaced with cooperation and coordination. Ironically, forty years earlier, cooperative behavior and coordination had been judged to be not in the public interest. The Sherman Antitrust Act of 1890 prohibited all forms of cooperative behavior. Section 5 of the Act exempted complying firms from prosecution under the antitrust laws.[2]

While Sections 1 through 6 described the new institutional framework for the conduct of business in the United States, the key to President Roosevelt's policy initiative was contained in Section 7. In a nutshell, nominal wages would rise, prices would be stabilized, the work week would be shortened, and labor would receive the right to bargain collectively. Each industry would set its own (*i*) minimum wage, (*ii*) length of work week, (*iii*) level of employment, and (*iv*) prices. The outcome would define the relevant industry-specific code of fair competition that would be submitted to the president for approval.

THE ORIGINS OF THE NIRA

While tariff policy had a long and productive history as a policy tool in U.S. economic history (Chapter 1), the proposed comprehensive, large-scale coordination of economic activity at the senior government level was unprecedented in peacetime. How, then, should the NIRA and the NRA be understood? Were there ideological and/or theoretical antecedents? According to the literature on the NRA and NRA, they were intellectual hodgepodges, not being based in any ideology or theoretical school. For example, historian Albert U. Romasco (1983) argued that the NIRA was a combination of a number of prevalent views at the time. A similar point was made by Leverett S. Lyon, Paul T. Homan, Lewis L. Lorwin, George Terborg, Charles L. Dearing, and Leon C. Marshall in *The National Recovery Administration: An Analysis and Appraisal*, according to whom the NIRA was the result of (1) economic planning (2) proposals for reorganizing American industry into vast monopolistic trusts under close government regulations (3) planning on an industry basis (4) predatory or destructive competition (5) technological unemployment and (6) current income in the hands of the masses being insufficient to carry out the market potential of the highly productive industrial system (1935, 6).

According to Romasco, the NIRA and NRA were created in the image and likeness of Roosevelt—in a word, eclectic. Describing Roosevelt's forays into policy making, he explains:

> Ideologically, Roosevelt and the New Deal were a no-man's land. Roosevelt's leadership and the New Deal had nothing to do with logic and consistency. Instead, Roosevelt used his position of power to carry out what was essentially an exercise in political eclecticism; he drew freely from a wide and contradictory variety of ideological programs both home grown and imported, and more often than not, he used them simultaneously. (Romasco 1983, 5)

While there is a grain of truth to this, the New Deal was not without a pedigree. The National Industrial Recovery Act was based largely on the work of two scholars, Professor Rexford G. Tugwell of Columbia University and Harold G. Moulton of the Brookings Institution. Rexford G. Tugwell had examined the electrification of U.S. industry in the 1910s and 1920s. America, he argued, was in the throes of a new industrial revolution (EHTCFPT's).[3] Like Henry Ford and Edward A. Filene, Tugwell's work was normative in nature. Getting in the way of accelerated growth was the failure of wage income to track the output of the consumption goods industries. Wages had not kept up with productivity, he argued. The electrification of U. S. industry had simply increased profits.

> But high wages are so necessary a condition of social progress that one, even, who is not a wage-earner might well argue for the strengthening of the workers' cause. For wages, more than any other income, are spent for staple goods, goods which, in the best sense, strengthen the race by their use. These too are the goods which can be made in the most efficient ways. But quite as important, income which is distributed as wages becomes immediate purchasing power for consumers goods, and so completes that productive circuit of which we have spoken. A nation of well-paid workers, consuming most of the goods its produces, will be as near Utopia as we humans are ever likely to get. It is necessary to this result that not too much income shall go to profits; for if it does, this will either be spent for wasteful luxuries which have to be made in extravagant ways, or will, if it is not spent, be distributed by bankers to enterprises who will over expand their productive facilities, forgetting that the worker's buying power is not sufficient to create a demand for them. (Tugwell 1933, 183)

Harold G. Moulton, President of the Brookings Institution, shared this view.[4] The failure of wage income to rise commensurately with productivity acted as a brake on economic growth.

> This diagnosis of the economic mechanism may then be summarized as follows. Our study of the productive process led us to a negative conclusion-no limiting factor or serious impediment to a full utilization of our productive capacity could be discovered. Our investigation of the distribution of income, on the other hand, revealed a maladjustment of basic significance. Our capacity to pro duce consumer goods has been chronically in excess of the amount which consumers are able, or willing, to take off the markets; and this situation is attributable to the increasing proportion of the total income which is diverted to the savings channels. The result is a

chronic inability-despite such devices as high pressure salesmanship, installment credits, and loans to facilitate foreign purchases-to find market outlets adequate to absorb our full productive capacity. (Moulton 1935, 46)

The solution: government-imposed wage increases. In *The Industrial Discipline and the Governmental Arts* (1933), Tugwell made the case for government control of wages and prices. In his view, markets and competition were inadequate.

Yet men have never been content with disorder. They have sought to plan and control. Often their institutions, to be sure, which were planned for one purpose, have prevented the achievement of another. Our Constitution is an illustration of this. It preserves certain rights, but it makes the preserving of others impossible. Then there is the inevitable lag of institutions behind changes in specific techniques. A social structure built slowly and piecemeal to provide for activities of one kind prevents, if the structure fails to change, activities of other kinds, and our institutions are so built into our regard that we award them the loyalty they have not deserved. (Tugwell 1933, 84)

Understandably, Tugwell became the chief target of the NIRA's opponents.[5] *The Industrial Discipline and the Governmental Arts* was the subject of much debate in the U.S. Senate from March to June 1933.

Clearly, the NIRA was not a hastily concocted piece of legislation, but rather, was based on a nineteenth-century intellectual tradition in economics, namely, the problem of underconsumption. Professor Tugwell's work ought to be included in this long and illustrious intellectual tradition.

Tugwell and Moulton's greatly influenced Senator Robert F. Wagner, the chief architect of the National Industrial Recovery Act.[6] In his defense of the proposed legislation, he referred to the wage problem in the following terms:

In my opinion, the depression arose in large part from failing to coordinate production and consumption. During the years, 1922-1929, corporate earnings rose much faster than wage rates. This led to an over expansion in productive equipment, particularly machinery and plant facilities. The great mass of consumers did not receive enough to take the goods off the market.[7]

Roosevelt echoed Wagner's concerns. In his message to Congress, just days before the act's final passage, he declared:

Before the special session of the Congress adjourns, I recommend two further steps in our national campaign to put people to work. My first request is that the Congress provide for the machinery for a great cooperative movement throughout industry in order to obtain wide reemployment, to shorten the workweek, to pay a decent wage for the shorter week, and to prevent unfair competition and disastrous over-production.[8]

The general consensus among members of the Administration was that unfettered competition had somehow failed (*Propositions 1* and *2*). Consider, for example, the views of Columbia University professor Adolf A. Berle, a prominent member of the celebrated "Brains Trust":

President Roosevelt's "New Deal" constitutes the introduction into the economic system of a new power of organization which can be used to counterbalance the effects of organization gone wrong and grant to every one economic security, a chance for self-fulfillment and a right to live. It is endeavoring, in a word, to make the tremendous collective organizations we have built up in the form of credit machinery corporations and the like, change from a dubious master into a faithful and honored servant. The new deal may be said to be merely a recognition of the fact that human beings cannot indefinitely be sacrificed by millions to the operation of the economic forces accentuated by this factor of organization. Further, the mere process of organization which could create the economic mechanism can be invoked to prevent the shocking toll on life and health and happiness which readjustment under modern conditions demands.... The forces that the "New Deal" called into action roughly correspond to the organized forces which economists recognize as the senior controls of our present society. The first and the most important is the control of credit banking currency. This, the most important, the most delicate and the most complex, was in obvious collapse on March 4. A second senior control lies in the tremendously concentrated domination of certain groups over industry. It was conceived that by mobilizing industry and requiring it to meet the responsibilities of an income-distributing group, much could be done towards achieving the balance and distribution of income which is required to keep a system like ours afloat.[9]

Like the Smoot-Hawley Tariff Bill of 1929, the NIRA enjoyed a considerable amount of support in the business community. Among the leading nonpartisan advocates of the NIRA was Henry I. Harriman, president of the U.S. Chamber of Commerce, who, on the day the bill became law, declared:

Today's passage of the N.I.R.A. constitutes a most important step in our progress towards business rehabilitation. It should begin immediately to bring about a large measure of reemployment and an increase in buying power throughout the country. The act itself will permit legitimate business enterprise to lift itself above the destructive competition which has prevented recovery and which has been threatening to bring about complete economic demoralization. With reasonable opportunity to work together, business enterprise might earlier have mitigated the effects of the depression. Continued denial of that opportunity, with a consequently great amount of business wreckage, would inevitably have renewed an era of mergers and combinations that followed earlier depressions and would have given rise to problems which the country, in the public interest, should be spared. This act now permits through voluntary agreements public benefits heretofore denied. The act will permit American firms, determined to protect American standards of living, from being forced through cutthroat competition to lower standards. An immediate and widespread participation by industry and commerce in the benefits supplied by the act will quickly put large numbers of men to work and will immediately act to spur business generally.[10]

THE NATIONAL RECOVERY ADMINISTRATION

Faced with the task of coordinating economic activity, the Roosevelt Administration created the National Recovery Administration (NRA) whose mandate consisted of (*i*) creating a regulatory body to oversee the day-to-day workings of the National Industrial Recovery Act, and (*ii*) to deal with all matters pursuant to national economic recovery. According to the NIRA, each industry would be required to draft a code dealing with such issues as wages, prices, employment, and hours. The NRA was an umbrella organization set up to oversee the drafting of and the management of these codes.

As it turns out, despite its rather swift passage through Congress, recovery as outlined in the NIRA would be long and protracted over time. Individual firms in industries would have to meet and agree on wages, prices, hours, and employment. The resulting codes would then be submitted to the government for final approval. Because time was of the essence, the president took it upon himself to expedite matters by instituting a blanket code, known as the President's Reemployment Agreement, which called for a 15 percent across-the-board increase in nominal wages. In *The ABC of The N.R.A.*, published in 1934, authors Charles L. Dearing, Paul T. Homan, Lewis L. Lorwin, and Leverett S. Lyon explained the President's actions as follows:

Moreover, during the first weeks after the passage of the Act, the idea of developing "mass purchasing power" through higher wages seems to have been prominent in the thinkings of official circles. To make the effects significantly large appeared to require more or less simultaneous extension of the principle of higher wages to large areas of industry. (Dearing *et al.* 1934, 60)

An Example: The Automobile Industry Code

Here, the Automobile Industry Code is examined in detail. Given its prominent role in the U.S. economy in the 1930s, the automobile industry figured prominently in the NIRA and NRA. In fact, discussions regarding the drafting of the "automobile code" commenced before the act was signed into law.

According to Sidney Fine (1963), the automobile industry expressed its views on the impending recovery bill early in April 1933, two months before its final enactment. The official position of the National Automobile Chamber of Commerce (NACC) on the NIRA was presented to the House Committee on Labor on May 5, 1933 by Alfred E. Sloan, president of General Motors. The NACC supported the proposed measures: "Most anything is justified that appears to offer a reasonable chance of relief." It objected, however, to its lack of flexibility, especially with regard to the "share-the-work" principle.

The automobile industry, Henry Ford notwithstanding, was favorable to the proposed legislation. Alfred Reeves, NACC vice-president, and Pyke Johnson, NACC's Washington representative, worked closely with General Hugh Johnson, director of the NRA. On June 15, 1933, the automobile industry informed Roosevelt and Johnson of its wish to cooperate "in getting men back to work." By June 22, 1933, the NACC code committee, presided by GM vice-president Donaldson Brown, received official approval. It would draft and administer the automobile industry code of fair competition.

The resulting code called for a maximum work week of 48 hours, with the annual average not exceeding 40 hours per week. Average hours were set at 35 per week. According to Sidney Fine:

> After examining the employment records of the NACC plants in the Detroit area and seeking the views of member firms outside the motor city, the committee decided to set the maximum weekly hours for covered factory employees at forty-eight and to stipulate that working hours averaged on an annual basis should not exceed forty per week. When it was deter-

mined, however, that the code should run only until December 31 and thus apply to a period of the year when production would be low, it was agreed that the average hours should be set at thirty-five per week from the effective date to the expiration date. (Fine 1963, 51)

Fine described the wage provisions of the code as follows:

> The committee decided that the minimum wage of adult male factory workers should be 40 cents per hour in cities less than 250,000 population, 41.5 cents in cities with populations of 250,000 to 500,000, and 43 cents in cities of over 500,000 populations. A five-cent differential was specified for female employees and for male factory workers under twenty-one; and the labor *of* children under sixteen years of age was entirely prohibited.... The minimum wage of office and salaried employees was set at $14.00 or $14.50 per week depending on the size of the community in which they worked. No provision was made for the adjustment of wages above the minimum. (Fine, 1963, 52)

That no provisions were made for adjusting wages above the minimum was common in the drafting of industry codes. Minimum wages, and not average wages, were set. Clearly, if an industry's wages exceeded the various minimum standards set by the NRA, then the code's wage provisions were virtually useless. Such was the case in the automobile industry. According to Fine, "90 per cent of NACC male employees were receiving more than 43 cents per hour at the end of June 1933, and the pay increases put into effect in July and August 1933, before the code was approved, increased this number to 95 per cent" (1963, 53).

SUCCESS OR FAILURE?

By 1935, 546 codes of fair competition had been approved, as well as 185 supplementary codes. In total, 22 million workers were covered. Wage and hour provisions varied by industry; however, each contained a minimum wage and various restrictions on the number of hours worked. Did the NIRA achieve its goals? Did it increase income and employment?

Before turning to these questions, it is important to point out that the NIRA was heuristic in nature. No one knew what the full-employment real wage was. No one knew what the appropriate wage was in each of the thousands of U.S. industries. No one knew where potential U.S. GNP stood. Most importantly, no one knew why real wages had failed to track productivity.

Leverett S. Lyon, Paul T. Homan, Lewis L. Lorwin, George Terborg, Charles L. Dearing and Leon C. Marshall described the NIRA as follows:

> When one has canvassed the sources of information, the conviction grows that those most closely concerned with drafting or sponsoring the act had themselves vague ideas of what was to be done, and not to be done, under it; and what administrative organization and procedure could effect its purposes while observing its limitations. In some degree, all these viewpoints noted as one seem to have touched the inner circle. There was doubtless substantial agreement that the lowest wages were to be raised, that the total wage bill was to be increased, and that available work was to be spread among more workers. Beyond that, each person had his own ideas of what should be done. There is some evidence of an official view that when industrial groups had come in and displayed their troubles it would be soon enough to determine what should be done. So far as can be learned, even the Administration had no idea to what extent it was fostering a modification or impairment of the familiar outlines of the system of the free enterprise system. (Lyon *et al.* 1935,25)

What was known, however, was that (*i*) the U.S. economy had been beset by chronic oversupply for some time, (*ii*) wages had not tracked productivity, and (*iii*) the U.S. economy was operating significantly below capacity.

> In the most general sense, there seems to have been a more or less official recovery theory based upon three hypotheses: (1) That an increase in payrolls would add to net current spending; (2) that raising the lowest wages would both promote spending, as just states, and in addition restore a proper balance between occupations which the depression had broken down; and (3) that measures which prevented further price declines, or in some cases raised prices, would create a state *of* business confidence favorable to forward commitments. (Lyon *et al.* 1935,26)

Table 6.1
U.S. Wage and Price Data—Manufacturing 1923-1945 [*]

Year	Wage	CPI	Real Wage
1923	0.52	51.3	1.01
1924	0.54	51.2	1.05
1925	0.54	51.9	1.04
1926	0.54	51.1	1.04
1927	0.54	50.0	1.08
1928	0.56	50.8	1.10
1929	0.56	50.6	1.10
1930	0.55	49.3	1.11
1931	0.51	44.8	1.13
1932	0.44	40.2	1.09
1933	0.44	39.3	1.11
1934	0.53	42.2	1.25
1935	0.54	42.6	1.26
1936	0.55	42.7	1.28
1937	0.62	44.5	1.39
1938	0.62	43.9	1.41
1939	0.63	43.2	1.45
1940	0.66	43.9	1.50
1941	0.73	47.2	1.54
1942	0.85	53.0	1.60
1943	0.96	56.8	1.69
1944	1.01	58.2	1.73
1945	1.02	59.7	1.70

[*]   Source: U.S. Department of Commerce (1975), Series D802, F5.

According to Roosevelt, the NIRA was directly responsible for the creation of four million jobs. General Hugh Johnson, however, offered a more conservative estimate, placing the number at 2.785 million jobs. Economists at the Brookings Institution put the number at 1.5 million. Furthermore, while nominal wages increased by between nine and ten percent, real wages actually decreased five to six percent the result of higher prices.

Wage data (Table 6.1) show that the nominal hourly wage in manufacturing went from $.44 in 1932 to $.54 in 1935. The consumer price index went from 40.20 in 1932 to 42.60 in 1935. The resulting real wage went from $1.09 in 1932 to $1.26, an increase of 15 percent. Clearly, the NIRA was successful, if only partially. Recall that no specific real-wage target had been set. Clearly, the NIRA fell short of its ultimate objective of industrial recovery. Unemployment remained high in 1935 and investment expenditure low.

This contrasts with the view that the NIRA, by preventing downward wage and price adjustment, made matters worse (Friedman and Schwartz 1963; Weinstein 1980; Temin 1990; Bernanke 1986,1994; Roose 1954; Hawley 1976). Accordingly, the Great Depression was the result of an important monetary contraction in the late 1920s (Temin) and early 1930s (Friedman and Schwartz). Recovery required wage and price deflation. The NIRA, by raising wages and stabilizing prices, hindered recovery, thus prolonging the depression. In *Recovery and Redistribution under the NIRA* (1980), Michael Weinstein estimated that the NIRA eliminated a potential eight percent average annual increase in real output that might otherwise have resulted from the monetary expansion of the NIRA period. Moreover, he asserted, it added another two percent to unemployment. According to Milton Friedman and Anna Schwartz:

> In his detailed analysis of the revival, Kenneth Roose quite plausibly attributes the unusually low levels of private investment at that time mainly to the effects of governmental policies. Those policies tended to make profits relatively low. Wage rises were promoted first through the N.I.R.A. codes and then, when the codes were declared unconstitutional in 1935, through the National Labor Relations Act and the enactment of minimum wage laws. (Friedman and Schwartz 1963, 495)

Interestingly, there is no mention of its objectives, its preamble, its theoretical foundations. Technology shocks, productivity, wages, income, savings, and profits are altogether absent from this literature. The most recent example is Peter Temin's "Socialism and Wages in the Recovery from the Great Depression in the United States and Germany" (1990) where the NIRA is examined in terms of the efficiency wage. While the analysis differs, the conclusion is essentially the same, namely, that "employment in the United States was restricted by high wages, which government policy raised above the level of efficiency wages" (Temin 1990, 297).

In 1935, the NIRA was declared unconstitutional and revoked, ending one of the most ambitious and far-reaching experiments in macroeconomic management-coordination in the history of Western industrial democracies.[11] This raises a number of "what-ifs." What if it had not been struck down? What if wages had continued to rise throughout the mid-to-late 1930s? Would output and employment have increased? Was the Roosevelt administration on the right track?

HENRY FORD AND THE NIRA

Ironically, Henry Ford opposed the NIRA and the NRA. While he shared its objectives, he bitterly opposed the means, namely government-imposed coercive cooperation. Ford refused to sign the automobile code. According to Sidney Fine (1963), his opposition stemmed from Section 7(a) of the NIRA regarding workers' rights, the closed shop principle and collective bargaining.

With the benefit of hindsight, the conflict opposing Ford, the NIRA, and Roosevelt had more to do with form than substance. Philosophically, Henry Ford shared more with Rexford G. Tugwell, Robert F. Wagner and Franklin D. Roosevelt than he did with his fellow businessmen. They all felt that purchasing power had to increase commensurately with America's capacity to produce. Wages had to rise, they argued. In fact, one could go as far as arguing that Ford was the first true "New Dealer," having anticipated the wage provisions of the NIRA by two decades.[12] The wage increases contained in Ford's five-dollar day in 1914, six-dollar day in 1919 and seven-dollar day in 1932 dwarfed those found in all 546 codes of fair competition. Philosophically, Ford opposed government infringement in American life in general. Businessmen, he argued, should spontaneously (in violation of *Proposition 1*) increase wages for the collective good (increasing ω_m). Despite having been ignored for over two decades, Ford continued throughout the 1930s to plead with his fellow businessmen to increase wages. As the following passage indicates, he clearly and naively preferred voluntary increases to government-imposed ones:1

We've got to stop that gouging process if we want to see all of the people reasonably prosperous. There is only one rule for industrialists and that is: Make the best quality of goods possible at the lowest cost paying the highest wages possible. Nothing can be right in this country until wages are right. The life of business comes forth from the people in orders. The factories are not stopped for lack of money but for lack of orders. Money loaned at the top means nothing. Money spent at the bottom starts everything. I think that if industrial leaders had been willing to push wages up and up during the last thirty years the present economic ills would at least not be as great as they are. If the government can help in these matters, well and good, but the government has not a rosy record in running itself thus far. [13]

PROFITS IN THE 1920S

The National Industrial Recovery Act of 1933 was the result of (*i*) the presence of substantial excess capacity in the 1920s, (*ii*) the apparent failure of wage income to track productivity, and (*iii*) the widespread belief that profits had increased at the expense of wages. The electrification of U.S. industry had increased capacity and productivity greatly. Wage income, however, had failed to rise creating a glut of consumption goods/capacity. Profit income, argued Tugwell, Moulton, Wagner and others, had increased throughout the 1920s at the expense of wage income.[15] The surplus generated by the adoption of continuous-flow mass-production techniques, they argued, had been captured entirely by capital. According to Rexford G. Tugwell:

> The picture of the modern industrial situation which must be carried in any honest and informed mind is one of a very mixed sort. Technique itself is having certain clear evolutionary movements. The main one, to which attention has been called here, is that of a double concentration and elaborative process. But this process has not been carried forward evenly. And it has built up new social groups which, while they exploited its new possibilities, have clung dogmatically to the theory of an outworn system of institutions. This happens, of course, because the active exploiters found that so long as the public could be persuaded to keep its eyes on an idealized picture, their own real activities, not being understood, could go on without much if any hampering control. Incidentally, this lack of control has made it possible for them to divert to their own uses, the greater share of the increased economic surpluses created by the new improvements. (Tugwell 1933, 85)

Theoretically, if productivity rises by τ percent and if capital captures all of the resulting increase in income, then it stands to reason that broadly-defined profits should rise by τ percent, where n is the share of profits in national income. For example, if n = 0.30, then with a value of τ of 0.40 would increase profits by 133 percent. If EHTCFPT increased productivity by 40 percent, then profits as a share of U.S. income should (n=0.30) leap from 30 to 50 percent.

Table 6.2
Functional Distribution of U.S. National Income, 1915-1939 [*]

Period	COMP	IUE	REN	CP	NI
1915-1924	57.2	21.0	7.6	8.9	5.3
1920-1929	60.5	17.6	7.6	8.2	6.2
1925-1934	63.0	15.8	6.6	6.4	8.1
1920-1939	66.8	15.0	5.0	4.9	8.2

[*] *Source:* U.S. Department of Commerce (1975), series F 186-191.

Income distribution data for the 1920s, however, fail to show any such "leap" in profits. Robert E. Keller (1973), for example, found that in 1923, employee compensation as a percentage of net income originating in manufacturing stood at 77.6 percent, while in 1929, it stood at 75.3 percent. For the economy as a whole, it stood at 77.9 percent in 1923 and 72.0 percent in 1929. Table 6.2 reports the functional distribution of income for various period intervals as reported by the U.S. Bureau of Economic Analysis. "Compensation of employees" (*COMP*) as a percentage of total income in the period 1925-1934 actually increased relative to 1920-1929 and 1915-1924. Clearly, profit income (*CP*) did not experience anything resembling the "leap" predicted by Tugwell, Moulton, Wagner and others.[16]

UNDERINCOME, THE NIRA AND THE BLUE EAGLE PROGRAM

The model presented in Chapter 2 constitutes a first of sorts. The Schelling-type coordination game is the first attempt at formalizing the myriad issues raised by the architects of the National Industrial Recovery Act of 1933. The

NIRA has, for the most part, been studied using what we consider to be inappropriate models, models whose premises are orthogonal to the underlying concerns of Senator Robert F. Wagner, Rexford G. Tugwell and other members of the "Brains Trust."

The first signs that the U.S. economy was in the throes of a massive technology shock came in the mid-to-late 1920s when unemployment and output were both increasing. We saw in Chapter 4 that the problem of unemployment in the late 1920s is what alerted Senator Robert F. Wagner to the presence of a more serious problem, namely the failure of the U.S. economy to move to a higher equilibrium growth path. As the Ford Motor Company had done in the 1910s, numerous U.S. manufacturing firms were actually cutting employment. Electrification had increased productivity: what could be done yesterday with say 100 workers now only required 75. Calls for higher external tariffs on imported manufactures in 1928 can, as such, be understood as an attempt by U.S. firms to sell more of their output on the domestic market. Electrification had provided them with the wherewithal to serve a larger share of the national market. Had they been successful, profits, at least in the short run, would have increased substantially. Remember, output had increased, while costs had remained relatively constant, and, in most cases, decreased, as the experience at the Ford Motor Company clearly demonstrated. The Smoot-Hawley Tariff Bill of 1929, it therefore follows, should be seen as an attempt on the part of the Hoover administration to push the U.S. economy on to the higher equilibrium growth path defined by the new technology.

In addition to the events in the 1920s and 1930s, these results also provide a theoretical basis for the study of the NIRA and NRA.[13] Robert Wagner and the members of the celebrated "Brains Trust," we argue, were both right and wrong in their diagnosis of the problems plaguing the U.S. economy in the late 1920s. They were right to point out that wages had not tracked productivity (see Chapter 3). Clearly, wage income had lagged substantially behind productivity. They were wrong, however, to put the blame on the capital and profits. The owners of capital had not appropriated the resulting surplus for the simple reason that the electrification of U.S. industry had not resulted in an increase in aggregate income. As a decade, the 1920s can best be characterized as a period of income inertia.

This explains why investors and shareholders opposed the various excess-profit taxes imposed in the 1930s. For example, in 1936, the Roosevelt administration imposed an undistributed profits tax. The underlying idea was simple: the alleged higher profits of the 1920s, its proponents argued, had failed to find their way back into the economy in the form of expenditure (Bernstein 1987, 190). According to Roosevelt advisor Rexford G. Tugwell, the persistence of the depression was due to the lethargy of capital. However, as our results show, capital could not appropriate and had not appropriated the surplus generated by the technology shock. This explains why throughout the 1930s, business leaders and investors vigorously opposed this tax.

What is interesting to note, however, is the optimality of the proposed solution (i.e. raising wages). That profit income had not, in fact, increased was of no consequence to the proposed solution. The key to recovery, reasoned Wagner, lay in increasing wage income. As the results of our analysis clearly show, increasing wages was also the key to increasing profits owing in large measure to the fact that profits are a residual factor payment. Higher aggregate wages lead to higher aggregate profits. Perhaps this explains why enlightened businessmen such as Henry Ford and Edward A. Filene, not to mention Henry Harriman, the president of the U.S. Chamber of Commerce, strongly supported the high wage provisions of the NIRA. Collectively, higher wages, they surmised, would lead to higher profits.

Under the NIRA and NRA, cooperation was the key to the recovery. All firms would have to increase wages, stabilize prices, and reduce hours. Industries would submit codes of fair competition to the NRA for approval. Clearly, the task was colossal. In our model, all *2qm* firms are identical. Firms within industries have identical cost and revenue structures. Government intervention, it therefore follows, is easy to accomplish. A 40 percent across-the-board wage increase will solve the coordination failure.

It goes without saying that such was not the case in the 1930s. Industries differed greatly as did firms within the same industry. The technology shock (i.e. continuous-flow mass production) had not hit all industries identically. Furthermore, not all firms within any given industry had *Fordized*. Overall manufacturing productivity had increased, as indicated in Chapter 3. No one, however, knew which firms (industries) were more productive and which weren't. By April 1935, this had become painfully obvious. According to Leverett S. Lyon, Paul T. Homan, Lewis L. Lorwin, George Terborg, Charles L. Dearing and Leon C. Marshall:

> Even though intentions may have been of the best, it remains clear that with few exceptions, the handling of the clauses governing wages above the minimum was and is inept. In the main, N.R.A. seems to have plunged into legislative and administrative action in this field with few facts for

guidance; with few comprehensive or definite policies ever formulated; and with little knowledge of the practical outcome-these are serious handicaps in any undertaking, but especially in one of such a complex and far-reaching character as the N.R.A. If wages above the minimum should be subjected to regulation by the federal government-a question which we may for the moment leave open-it goes without saying that some better means of control is needed than the present code provisions afford. (Lyon *et al.* 1935, 364)

Ideally, what was needed were detailed firm-specific and industry-specific data on productivity and/or electric power consumption. Wages at either the firm or industry levels, it therefore follows, would have been adjusted accordingly. For example, if productivity increased by 30 percent, then real wages would have been increased by 30 percent.

MONITORING COSTS

Legally speaking, the NIRA fell under the jurisdiction of the Federal Trade Commission. According to the *Congressional Record* of June 7, 1933:

> Violation of any of the provisions of the code by anyone engaged in interstate commerce, or business affecting interstate commerce, constitutes unfair competition and subjects the violator to an order by the Federal Trade Commission to cease and desist from his unfair practices. Such violation is also a misdemeanor and the offender is subject to a fine of $500 for each day of violation. A Code may be enforced by injunction proceedings in Federal Courts.[14]

Clearly, the costs of policing the hundreds of codes of fair competition would be astronomical. A veritable army of civil servants would be required. To circumvent this problem, Robert F. Wagner and NRA chief, General Hugh Johnson, devised an ingenious cooperation-enforcing device, namely, the Blue Eagle program. Firms that signed their respective industry code (i.e. those who raised wages and stabilized prices) would be allowed to display a Blue Eagle on their products. A massive publicity campaign encouraging Americans to patronize complying firms and boycott "cheating" ones was then mounted. Analytically, the Blue Eagle program *de facto* internalized the cost of not complying (i.e. cheating) to non-complying firms.[15] With the support of American consumers, it upped the ante: non-complying firms ran the risk of losing some, if not ail, of their customer base.

As pointed out, Henry Ford refused to sign the automobile code. As such, Ford automobiles could not bear the Blue Eagle or, as he referred to it, the "Roosevelt buzzard." Ford became a symbol of opposition to government regulation and collectivism. Many supporters of the NIRA and NRA wanted the federal government to "put Ford in his place." According to Sidney Fine, because Ford complied with the automobile code, there was little it could do. Its only recourse, as it turned out, was the Blue Eagle. For example, at his press conference of August 29, 1933, Hugh Johnson, when asked if he intended to crack down on Ford, replied: "I think that maybe the American people will crack down on him when the Blue Eagle is on other cars and he does not have one" (Fine 1963, 79).

A NEW SOCIAL ORDER

As we have shown, in times of radical technological change, competition is welfare-reducing. Technology shocks do not lead to higher output, income and expenditure. There are no private incentives to increase wages commensurately with productivity. Instead, what is required is nothing short of a paradigm change in behavior. Specifically, in times of massive technology shocks, firms must somehow cooperate.

This conclusion was shared by, among others, Professor Rexford G. Tugwell and Boston businessman Edward A. Filene, both of whom called for the creation of a new social order.[16] Both were adamant: the existing economic order was in need of change. For example, Filene doubted whether the profit motive as modeled above served the "common welfare." While not advocating its outright abolition, he saw room for change. It is perhaps important to remember that Filene was a businessman by profession, and not a social reformer. Filene believed that profits could only rise if wages rise. In his words:

> The time has come, however, when the greatest total profits can be secured only through supplying the masses with the best values. So there is no war now between selfishness and unselfishness; the only war is between the traditional notion of where self-interest lies and the newly discovered truths of profit-making. (Filene 1931,201)

Clearly, what Filene was implying is that "to make money, one has to spend money." Given the massive technology shock that resulted from electrification of U.S. industry, firms had to increase wages in order to increase profits.[17] In such times, Filene argued, cooperation dominates competition.

Rexford G. Tugwell was of a similar persuasion. Like Henry Ford and Edward A. Filene, he believed firmly that the traditional profit motive was inadequate. However, unlike the eternally-optimistic Ford and Filene who continued to plead with fellow businessmen to increase wages and lower prices, Tugwell saw the need for change. Acutely aware of the nature of the problem (i.e. the prisoner's dilemma), he advocated third-party intervention in the form of "institutional reorganization" and "controlled planning." Only by reorganizing industry, he argued, could the "potentialities of technique" be released. in hindsight, it is clear that he was right: private wage-setting competitive economies cannot make the nominal transition to the higher equilibrium growth path defined by the technology shock.

What differentiates Tugwell, on the one hand, from Ford and Filene, on the other, are their views on the underlying nature of cooperation. Tugwell favored mandatory (i.e. government-imposed) cooperation. Governments ought to set wages and prices. Ford and Filene favored voluntary cooperation. Businessmen ought to raise wages for their good, and the good of society. Similarly, Republican President Herbert C. Hoover and Democratic Senator Robert F. Wagner, who were political adversaries, favored voluntary cooperation; General Hugh Johnson, the director of the NRA favored mandatory cooperation. All were reformers in their own right. Ford and Filene sought to change the very ethos of the twentieth-century businessman, while Tugwell and Johnson attempted to change the institutional framework in which business was conducted. Biographer Michael Namorato described Rexford G. Tugwell's view of man in general and businessmen in particular as follows:

> As an institutional economist, Tugwell believed that man, although incapable of altering his nature, could change his environment. in doing so, he also had to adjust his thinking so as to reap the full benefits of those changes. When he refused to do so, a cultural lag or imbalance developed, as had happened in the United States. What happened is that as technology increased America's productive potential, American values remained constant. Social and political institutions failed to adapt to the complexity of modern life, so America fell behind the technology that was being developed. (Namorato 1988, 48)

All, however, shared one basic belief, namely, that the solution to the problem facing the U.S. economy in the 1920s and the 1930s lay in cooperation.

Wages and wage income would have to rise in step with productivity. Then and only then would profits and profit income increase. Some favored voluntary cooperation, while others called for government intervention.

REAL TRANSITIONS

Thus far, we have assumed that the $2n$ prices in our model are fixed. Let us now consider the case in which prices are downwardly flexible. Theoretically, this is not unreasonable in light of the fact that extremely-high-throughput, continuous-flow mass production techniques, by increasing productivity, lowered per-unit costs. Suppose that in our hypothetical economy, all firms decreased prices by 40 percent. It follows that real wage income and real profit income would rise by 40 percent, *ceteris paribus*. The economy would, as a result, move from the lower to the higher equilibrium growth path defined by the technology shock.[18]

This raises a number of questions. For example, why did prices in the 1920s not fall? Why did more cost-efficient firms resist price cuts? in this section, we describe a number of potential obstacles. For example, as pointed out in Chapter 4, EHTCFPT-induced cost savings in the 1920s could only be achieved at full capacity. Hence, a necessary condition for lower prices is increased sales and output. Full capacity, it turns out, requires price reductions (i.e. in order to increase real income). Few were the managers in the 1920s who were prepared to reduce price in anticipation of the resulting lower unit costs. Henry Ford was the exception. Throughout the 1910s and 1920s, he reduced the price of FMC products, and invited his fellow businessmen to do likewise. His message fell on deaf ears. The historical record shows that firms in the 1920s, despite substantial productivity gains, did not lower their prices.

Rexford G. Tugwell made a similar point. According to biographer Michael Namorato, he believed that:

> Business would only lower prices only when there was a promise of full continuity in the productive process. In light of the individualistic character of American industry, this meant that businessmen reduced prices only if and when they were certain that consumers would buy more of their products and not their competitors. (Namorato 1988, 48)

This raises the possibility of a second coordination failure. If all firms lower their prices, real income increases, increasing sales, and lowering costs. However, if just one lowers its price, it may fail to increase sales sufficiently to justify the lower price.[19] As was the case in the nominal transition, government intervention could, at least theoretically, correct this coordination failure. For example, the government could legislate a 40 percent decrease in all prices, which would, *ceteris paribus*, lead to a 40 percent increase in the real wage, real wage income, real consumption, real profits and real investment. Whether businessmen in the 1920s would have opposed such a plan, however, is open to question. It is my view that businessmen in the 1920s would have in all likelihood seen a 40 percent reduction in prices as resulting in a 40 percent reduction in nominal profits. This, of course, raises the question of money illusion: were businessmen and shareholders of the 1920s maximizing real or nominal profits? Clearly, a 40 percent reduction in prices would have (assuming a unitary elastic aggregate demand curve for consumption goods), resulted in constant nominal profits, but a 40 percent increase in real profits. Judging from the business community's obsession with stemming price deflation in the early 1930s, there is little doubt in my mind that government-imposed price deflation in the 1920s would not have found the favor of the average businessman.

OTHER SOLUTIONS

As the analysis has shown, the main obstacle to achieving a successful nominal transition is the presence of income inertia, both nominal and real. The technology shock increases productive capacity without increasing income. Wages fail to increase largely because profits fail to increase, labor being a derived demand. Profits fail to increase because income fails to increase. Consider the following solutions to the problem of income inertia. First, suppose that capital were paid a productivity-based dividend in much the same way as labor is paid a wage-that is, before firms' total sales are known. Recall that according to our model, factor payments to capital are a residual. That is, they are paid in the form of dividends once earnings are realized.

In the case of our hypothetical economy, the consumption goods sector dividend would be $40.8 billion dollars, while the capital goods sector dividend would be $22 billion. Total nominal income would, as such, be $179.5 billion. Technology shocks, by increasing total output, would raise total income. The consumption-goods sector dividend would rise by $46.6 to $87.5 billion, while the capital-goods sector dividend would rise by $25.2 to $47.2 billion.[20] Total expenditure would increase as a result.

Another way around this indeterminacy consists of remunerating electric power on the basis of its productivity. As the experience at the Ford Motor Company clearly illustrates, electric power increased productivity substantially. While income at the FMC increased as the result of the five-dollar day, it failed to increase in the economy as a whole. Theoretically, one could argue that the electrification of U.S. industry in this period generated rents. Specifically, the marginal revenue product of electric power exceeded its price. Suppose that electric power utilities priced their product on a productivity basis. In this case, the price of electric power would increase substantially. Since firms finance the purchase of electric power" in the same way they finance purchases of labor, namely via bank credit, it stands to reason that income would rise. For example, by attributing the 40 percent increase in output referred to above to electric power, total revenue of the electric power industry would have risen by $71.8 billion. Electrification would have cost each of the 50,000 consumption goods firms an additional $932,800, and each of the 50,000 capital goods firms, $503,200 which represents 40 percent of their respective total revenue and 61.5 percent of total variable costs. Total income (nominal and in kind) would, as such, have risen by 40 percent (i.e. by $71.8 billion). The key in this case is that electric power costs are not a residual in the way payments to capital are. In such a world, firms intent on adopting extremely-high-throughput, continuous-flow mass-production techniques would increase output and income.

Conclusion

As was shown in this chapter, private wage—and price-setting Nash economies, by their very nature, cannot make the transition from one equilibrium growth path to another in response to major technology shocks. Individual firms have no private incentives to increase wages commensurately with productivity. The problem, it was argued, is best modeled as a classical prisoner's dilemma. Non-cooperative behavior on the part of wage-setting firms leads to second-best outcomes, in this case, underincome.

It was argued that such a prisoner's dilemma characterized the U.S. economy in the 1920s, leading two successive administrations (i.e. Hoover and Roosevelt) to take extraordinary measures to literally push the U.S. economy on to the new, higher equilibrium growth path defined by the new technology. Clearly, neither President Hoover (Senator Smoot) or President Roosevelt (Senator Wagner) understood the intricacies of prisoner's dilemmas and underincome, which explains, at least in part, the failure of both policy measures. This being said, it must be pointed out that, theoretically-speaking, Hoover's plans for an associative state based on non-coercive interfirm cooperation, and *Wagner's National Industrial Recovery Act*, were both years ahead of their time, as evidenced by their total absence in contemporary economics. In the next chapter, estimates of overproduction and underincome in the U.S. economy during the 1920s, 1930s and 1940s are presented.

7

The Smoot-Hawley Tariff Act:
Too Little, Too Late, Too Much
to Ask...?

The evidence is overwhelming, not to mention damning: Willis C. Hawley, Reed Smoot and the Republican party were in over their heads. To believe that import substitution in what at the time was a closed economy (U.S. in the 1920s) could correct what was a fundamental disequilibrium, the result of the "greatest" process technology shock of all time (electrification) bordered on folly. To suggest that a policy that had, after over a century of application had virtually closed the U.S. economy to foreign trade, could be counted on to close what was a "chasm" between potential and actual output, one that widened throughout the 1920's, was to be disturbingly I.

This chapter puts the Smoot-Hawley Tariff Act in perspective. To this end, we begin by presenting estimates of the gap separating actual and potential output—that is, the gap between potential output as defined by the new process technology, and actual output. We then present U.S. export and import data for the period in question. This provides the wherewithal to evaluate the feasibility of import substitution as a means of addressing the problem of underincome. This is followed by the game-theoretical aspects of Smoot-Hawley in a multi-country context. Willis C. Hawley, Reed Smoot and the Republican party played what was a Nash strategy, raising tariffs. We then ask the question, is there evidence that either foresaw an eventual backlash? As pointed out in Chapter 5, European countries retaliated by raising tariffs, prompting an outright tariff war, the results of which included the breakdown of the world trade. This raises a number of questions. Was this an example of pure folly, or was it a "rational strategy?"

Estimating Potential U.S. GNP 1925-1944

The evidence presented thus far is unequivocal: the electrification of U.S. industry increased conventionally-defined productivity, productive capacity, and overall potential output. However, the failure of income to rise in step with potential output led to conditions of generalized oversupply, the Smoot-Hawley Tariff Bill, the stock market boom and crash, and the Great Depression. Questions, however, remain. While Henry Ford, Edward A. Filene, Rexford G. Tugwell, Robert F. Wagner and countless others pointed to oversupply in the 1920s as the cause of the Great Depression, none provided estimates of potential U.S. gross national product, nor of the gap between it and actual gross national product. Where, for example, did potential U.S. GNP stand throughout the 1920s and 1930s?

In this chapter, we present a series of measures of potential U.S. GNP from 1925 to 1944. Given the shortcomings of the existing techniques for measuring potential GNP in times of paradigm technological change, new techniques were developed and applied. The first is based on equilibrium growth theory. in short, estimates of potential GNP and τ, the technology shock (in percent), from 1925 to 1944 are obtained by choosing a terminal year at which potential GNP and actual GNP are assumed equal and extrapolating backward at the rate of growth of the labor supply. This provides estimates of potential GNP for all years prior to the chosen terminal year. The second technique is based on reported labor productivity growth, the idea being that labor productivity growth is a proxy for the rate of technological change (i.e. Hicks-neutral and/ or Harrod-neutral). The third and fourth techniques infer τ, the economy-wide rate of productivity growth, by examining long-run developments in factor markets, specifically in the labor market and the stock market.

MEASURING POTENTIAL GNP

Measures of potential GNP play a pivotal role in macroeconomics. For example, they allow for estimates of excess capacity and unemployment, two key macroeconomic variables. Likewise, they provide estimates of forgone opportunities. If the unemployment rate stands at ten percent, then one can conclude that society forgoes five to ten percent of potential GNP. Not surprisingly, economists have developed a number of measures of potential GNP. For example, there are estimates of potential GNP based on a straight application of Okun's Law. in the 1960s, Arthur Okun found a relatively stable relationship between output and employment. Specifically, for each percentage point by which the unemployment rate is above the natural rate, real potential GNP is three percent below potential GNP. Unemployment and GNP time-series data, it therefore follows, can be used to construct a measure of potential GNP.[1] A second approach consists of simply identifying peaks in actual GNP and joining them with straight lines which serve as measures of potential GNP. The Wharton School Index is one such index.

Problems, however, arise when measuring potential GNP in periods of paradigm technological change using these two approaches. Both yield biased estimates of potential GNP. For example, the electrification of U.S. industry altered fundamentally the relationship between output and employment. A straight application of Okun's law, it therefore follows, will inevitably yield downwardly-biased estimates. The Wharton School Index of potential GNP implicitly assumes that technological change results in an increase in actual GNP. As shown in Chapter 2, private wage and price-setting Nash economies, by their very nature, fail to make the transition (solve the coordination problem) to higher equilibrium growth paths in response to a technology shock.[2] Potential GNP in this case will exceed measured potential GNP owing to technology shocks.

In the face of these problems, we opted for an alternative approach, namely, backward extrapolation, a technique that is based on equilibrium growth theory. Growth theory maintains that gross national product grows at rate of $n + \tau$, where n is the rate of labor force growth and τ is the rate of Hicks-neutral or Harrod-neutral technological change (i.e. measured in productivity terms). It being the case that positive, occurrences of τ do not necessarily translate into contemporaneous growth prevents us from measuring technological change by using actual GNP data for the year(s) in question. However, let us assume that while positive τ values do not result in contemporaneous growth, they do, nonetheless, eventually work themselves into the growth rate, and hence, into actual GNP. It then follows that by identifying such a point in time, estimates of potential GNP for all preceding years can be obtained by extrapolating actual GNP for the year in question back in time at the rate of growth of the labor supply.

For example, suppose that the U.S. economy had solved the underlying coordination failure (*Proposition 2* in Chapter 2) by 1944. That is, by 1944, the

U.S. economy had reached its full potential. Potential GNP for all years prior to 1944 can be estimated by simply discounting 1944 actual GNP by the rate of growth of the labor force. In 1944, U.S. GNP stood at $361.3 billion. The rate of growth of the U.S. non-agricultural labor force from 1910 to 1950 was estimated at 1.85 percent per annum. Potential 1925 GNP, it therefore follows, can be obtained by dividing $361.3 billion by 1.4166404 (i.e. $(1.0185)^{19}$), the appropriate discount factor, which yields $255.0 billion. Dividing the former by the level of actual 1925 U.S. GNP of $179.4 billion yields a value for τ of 0.4216. That is, the resulting estimate of τ, the technology shock, in this case is 42.1 percent.

The same reasoning can be applied to productivity and wage data. For example, productivity estimates in 1943 relative to 1925 can be used to infer τ values. Similarly, real wage data in 1943 relative to 1925 can be used to infer τ values. Altogether, four techniques were used to estimate potential GNP and τ values for the period 1925 to 1944. The first three are based on backward extrapolation, while the fourth simply infers τ values from stock price movements in the 1920s.

EQUILIBRIUM GROWTH THEORY-BASED ESTIMATES OF POTENTIAL GNP

Table 7.1
Backward Extrapolation Estimates of Potential U.S. Gross National Product-Unweighted

| | Target Year (t") | | |
Base Year (t')	1925	1927	1929
1943	242.3	251.4	260.7
	(.3508)	(.3245)	(.2809)
1944	255.0	264.5	274.4
	(.4216)	(.3938)	(.3164)

1. Base and target years are reversed owing to the nature of the corresponding estimates (i.e. backward looking).

2. Actual *U.S. GNP*/$(1+n)^{1.085(20)}$.

3. Potential *U.S. GNP*/actual *U.S. GNP*—1 (billion constant 1958 dollars).

The first set of estimates of potential U.S. GNP and resulting values for τ, the technology shock, was obtained by applying standard growth theory. Growth theory predicts that equilibrium GNP grows at rate $n + \tau$ in periods of technological change (Hicks-neutral and Harrod-neutral) and at rate n otherwise, where n is the rate of labor force growth.[3] It therefore follows that by identifying-or assuming-a value for t', the base year, such that the economy finds itself at full employment, potential GNP for all $t < t'$ can be obtained by discounting actual GNP at time t' by a factor $(1+n)^{t'-t''}$, where t'' corresponds to the target year (i.e. the time of the shock). Two base years (i.e. t'), notably 1944 and 1943, and three target years (i.e. t''), 1925, 1927 and 1929, were chosen.

The resulting matrix of potential U.S. GNP values and the corresponding τ values, is provided in Table 7.1. in 1943, real U.S. GNP was $337.1 billion (constant 1958 dollars), which, extrapolated backward to 1925 at an annual rate of 1.85 percent, yields a value for potential U.S. GNP in 1925 of $242.3 billion (see Figure 7.1).[4] That is, actual 1925 U.S. GNP of $242.3 billion growing at an annual rate of 1.85 percent, the rate of growth of the labor force, yields a level of 1943 U.S. GNP of $337.1 billion. Dividing this figure by reported actual 1925 GNP of $179.4 billion (constant 1958 dollars) provides a value of τ, the rate of technological change, of 0.3508 (reported in parentheses). By opting for 1944 as the relevant base year, potential 1925 U.S. GNP rises to $255.3 billion, which corresponds to a value for τ of 0.4216.

Figure 7.1
Actual and Potential U.S. Gross National Product, 1925-1945
(Weighted and Unweighted)

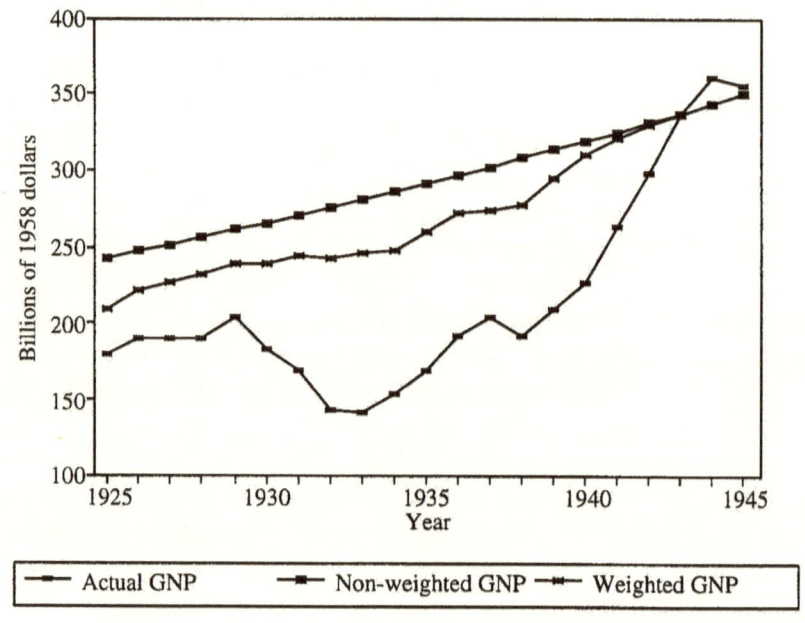

Source: U.S. Department of Commerce (1975), series F47

Taken together, potential U.S. GNP, as defined by the available production technology in 1925 (i.e. mass production), was between 35 $(t' = 1943)$ and 42 $(t' = 1944)$ percent greater than actual GNP (see Figure 7.1). Similarly, potential U.S. GNP in 1927 was between 23 $(t' = 1943)$ and 39 $(t' = 1944)$ percent greater than actual GNP, and lastly, potential GNP in 1929 was between 23 $(t' = 1943)$ and 34 $(t' = 1944)$ percent greater than actual GNP.

WEIGHTED ESTIMATES

These estimates are based on a number of assumptions, one of which being that the electrification of U.S. industry was instantaneous; that is, developments at the Ford Motor Company were instantaneously adopted throughout all sectors of the U.S. economy. Clearly, this is a strong assumption. It is a well-known fact that with all process innovations, big or small, there are significant diffusion lags. Firms may delay the application of the new technology to coincide with their investment cycle. Or conversely, firms may find themselves constrained on product markets, which will also lead to delays. Thus, it would be naive to assume that mass production instantaneously revolutionized U.S. industry. A more empirically-accurate assumption would be that it altered productivity and output over a period of time.

Table 7.2
Backward Extrapolation Estimates of Potential U.S. Gross National Product—Weighted

Base Year (t')	Target Year (t")		
	1925	1927	1929
1943	209.4 (.1675)	227.3 (.1979)	238.8 (.1729)
1944	215.5 (.2013)	235.3 (.2402)	247.2 (.2141)

1. Base and target years are reversed owing to the nature of the corresponding estimates (i.e. backward looking).

2. Actual U.S. $GNP/(1+n)^{1.085(20)}.$

3. Potential U.S. GNP/actual U.S. GNP—1 (billion constant 1958 dollars).

Figure 7.2
Estimates of the Gap between Actual and Potential U.S. Gross National Product, 1925-1945

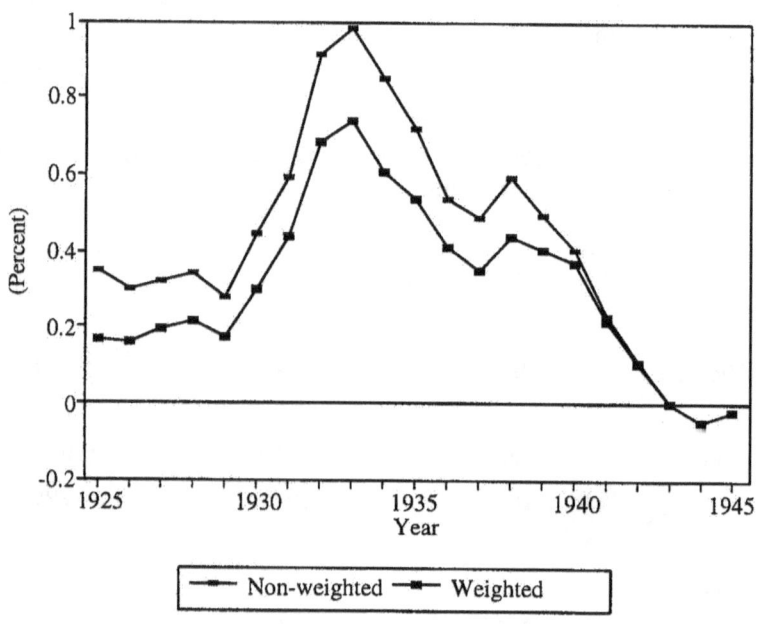

In light of this, a second set of estimates of potential GNP and τ, the technology shock, was generated. Using the diffusion index constructed in Chapter 3, we derived the matrix of weighted potential U.S. GNP values and τ values provided in Table 7.2. Specifically, the estimates of τ obtained in Table 7.1 were simply scaled by the diffusion index in Chapter 3. For example, unweighted potential 1925 U.S. GNP stands at $255.0 billion, which yields a τ value of 0.4216. According to Table 2.1, by 1925, EHTCFPT had penetrated roughly 47.7 percent of firms in the U.S. manufacturing sector. Multiplying the former by the latter results in a weighted estimate of τ of 0.20. Substantially lower estimates of potential GNP and τ now result. For example, weighted potential GNP in 1925 (base year 1944) stands at $215.5 billion (τ = .2013) as opposed to $255.0 billion (τ = .4216). in general, potential U.S. GNP, as defined by the production technology in place in 1925 (i.e. mass production), was between 16.7 *(t' = 1943)* and 20.1 *(t' = 1944)* percent greater than actual GNP. Moreover, potential U.S. GNP in 1927 was between 19.7 *(t' = 1943)* and 24.2 *(t' = 1944)* percent greater than actual GNP, and lastly, potential GNP in 1929 was between 17.2 *(t' = 1943)* and 21.4 *(t' = 1944)* percent greater than actual GNP (see Figure 7.2).

PRODUCTIVITY GROWTH-BASED ESTIMATES OF τ

The logic of backward extrapolation was also used to estimate aggregate and sector-specific values for τ: from reported labor productivity data from *t"* to *t'*. Specifically, by assuming that the underlying technology shock is Hicks-neutral, estimates of τ: were obtained by simply differencing labor productivity at times *t'* and *t"*.

The resulting set of estimates of τ: for all *t"* = 1924, 1925, and 1926, based on labor productivity growth data from 1924 to 1944, is presented in Table 7.3, where we see values for τ in manufacturing ranging from 80.3 percent (end-of-base year 1923 to end-of-target year 1944) to 58.9 percent (end-of-base year 1925 to end-of-target year 1944). For the U.S. economy as a whole, the values for τ range from 57.3 percent (1924-1944) to 51.0 percent (1926-1944).

LABOR MARKET-BASED ESTIMATES OF τ

At the center of the coordination failure described in Chapter 2 is the absence of private incentives to increase wages commensurately with productivity, either by raising individual nominal rates (*Proposition 1*) and/or reducing the price level. A number of events in the 1930s and early 1940s, however, contributed to increasing real wages. Chief among these were the National Industrial Recovery Act, the New Deal, and World War II-induced government expenditure. Here, by assuming that the resulting real wage (i.e. in 1945) reflected productivity more accurately, we inferred values for τ by comparing real wages in the mid-1940s with those in the 1920s.

First, we compared the real wage in manufacturing in 1944 to the real wage in 1924 (end-of-year 1923 data). Referring to Table 6.1 in Chapter 6, we see that the real wage in manufacturing between 1923 and 1944 increased 71 percent. The resulting estimate of τ would stand at 0.712.[5] The real wage in U.S. manufacturing at the end of 1923 stood at $1.01 (constant 1958 dollars); in 1944, it had increased to $1.73 (constant 1958 dollars). What is particularly interesting to note is the fact that the bulk of the increase came via an increase in the nominal wage, which increased from \$0.52 in 1923 to \$1.01 in 1944. The price level (1958=100) increased from 51.3 in 1923 to 58.2 in 1944.

Table 7.3
Labor Productivity-Based Estimates of τ [*]

	Base Year (t")					
Target Year(t')	1924		1925		1926	
	Total	Man.	Total	Man.	Total	Man.
1926	7.03	15.67	2.46	8.84	2.69	1.97
1928	8.89	23.63	4.26	16.12	4.49	8.99
1930	9.60	30.39	4.93	22.19	5.16	14.69
1932	6.32	25.62	1.79	17.99	2.02	10.74
1934	14.75	42.78	9.86	23.44	10.11	25.87
1936	24.59	53.23	19.28	43.92	19.55	35.08
1938	28.10	49.00	22.64	39.95	22.92	31.35
1940	37.00	70.89	31.16	61.51	31.46	50.65
1942	45.19	80.09	39.01	69.15	39.32	58.77
1944	57.37	80.34	50.67	69.39	51.01	58.99

[*]   Source: U.S. Department of Commerce (1975), Series D86 and D685

1.   End-of-year data.

2.   (Output per man-hour in t'-output per man-hour in t'')/output per man-hour in t'').

STOCK MARKET-BASED ESTIMATES OF τ

As was shown in Chapter 4, the stock market boom of 1928-1929 was the direct result of the Hoover administration's tariff initiative. By further restricting foreign firms' access to the U.S. market, the tariff hikes proposed in the Smoot-Hawley Tariff Bill would provide U.S. firms with a larger share of the domestic market. Sales, earnings, and profits, it was anticipated, would increase as a result. Investors reacted by bidding up the price of shares. According to basic financial analysis, the greater the anticipated increase in earnings, the greater the price increase. *Ceteris paribus*, if investors expected earnings to rise by τ percent, then stock prices should increase by an equivalent amount.[6]

This forms the basis of the estimates of τ, the technology shock, reported in this section. Specifically, we infer values for τ from stock-price movements in the period under consideration. We begin by examining in detail the relationship between a technology shock and expected earnings/dividends. Basic theory predicts that if the underlying technological change is of the Hicks-neutral variety, then both labor and capital productivity should increase commensurately, as both are more productive. Wages and dividends ought to increase accordingly. However, as shown in Chapter 2, there are no private incentives for firms to increase wages (*Propositions 1* and *2*). This raises an important question, namely how do investors in general, and investors in the 1920s in particular, see the relationship between technological change and real wages. For example, when estimating the earnings potential of the introduction of a new technology, do they factor in wage increases? Analytically, this amounts to asking whether investors play a Nash strategy as opposed to a rational strategy vis-à-vis wages. in other words, do they take the wage as given (i.e. the Nash strategy), or do they factor wage increases into expected earnings (i.e. the rational strategy)?

Admittedly, this is an empirical question. For investors to factor-in anticipated wage increases, it would have to be the case that in the past (i.e. historically), process innovations systematically led to real wage hikes; otherwise, there would be no reason to believe that investors would do so. On this note, the empirical evidence shows the absence of a one-to-one relationship between real wages and productivity. As was shown in Chapter 2, firms have no private incentives to increase real wages (*Proposition 1*). Moreover, the data show nominal and real wages in U.S. manufacturing to be constant throughout this period in spite of important productivity increases. It would therefore not be unreasonable to conclude that investors in the late 1920s played what amounted to a Nash strategy *vis-à-vis* wages.

This has important implications for the behavior of expected dividends and, hence, stock prices. For example, it implies that since the proportion of earnings-to-capital constitutes a fraction (i.e. roughly 30 percent) of total firm income, expected dividends would increase by more than τ percent. Specifically, they would increase by a multiple of τ. Consider the following numerical example. As in Chapter 6, let π define the ratio of capital income to total firm income. Suppose that $\pi = 0.3$. Hypothetical total firm income of $100 would yield factor payments to capital on the order of $30, which, capitalized at a rate of interest of 3 percent per annum, would yield a stock value of $1,000. Now, assume that τ takes on a value of 0.40. That is, the process innovation in question increases productivity by 40 percent. For a constant nominal wage, the resulting share value would rise to $2,333, as the anticipated $40 rise in earnings would be factored totally into share prices. The rate at which the hypothetical share price would rise is given as τ/π, which in this case corresponds to 1.33 (133 percent). Thus, what would in normal circumstances, be a 40 percent increase in share value is magnified by a factor of 3.325.

This simple technique was used to estimate τ_s, τ_m, τ_r, and τ_u, the implicit-in-share price technology shock in the economy as a whole, manufacturing (industrials), railroads and utilities, respectively, using the corresponding Standard and Poor's indexes of stock market prices from 1923 to 1929. Referring to Table 8.4, we see that total, industrial, railroad, and utilities real share prices increased some 238, 231, 102, and 230 percent, respectively, from 1924 to 1929. This implies that by 1929, initial hypothetical book value of $1,000 in each of these sectors would have risen to $3,380 for the market as a whole, $3,310 for manufacturing, $2,020 for railroads, and $3300 for utilities. For these to exist as financial market equilibria, anticipated sector earnings of $101.40, $99.30, $60.60 and $99.00 are required, which, when initial earnings of $30.00 are netted out, yield values for τ_s, τ_m, τ_r, and τ_u, of 71, 69, 31, and 69 percent, respectively.

Table 7.4
Stock Market-Based Estimates of τ, 1924-1929 [*]

1924-1929

Stock Index	1929	1923	Growth	
Total S&P	56.42	16.71	238	71
Industrials S&P	42.19	12.74	231	69
Industrials DJIA	352.51	95.52	269	81
Railroads S&P	91.27	45.13	102	31
Utilities S&P	117.25	35.30	230	69

1925-1929

Stock Index	1929	1923	Growth	
Total S&P	51.42	17.67	191	57
Industrials S&P	42.19	13.34	216	65
Industrials DJIA	352.51	120.51	192	57
Railroads S&P	91.27	48.86	87	26
Utilities S&P	117.25	37.79	210	63

1926-1929

Stock Index	1929	1923	Growth	
Total S&P	51.42	21.48	139	42
Industrials S&P	42.19	16.74	152	46
Industrials DJIA	352.51	156.66	125	37
Railroads S&P	91.27	57.63	76	23

Table 7.4
Stock Market-Based Estimates of τ, 1924-1929 (Continued)[*]

Utilities S&P	117.25	45.05	160	48

---

[*] Source: U.S. Department of Commerce (1975), series X-487-491; Pierce (1991).

The way to interpret these results is as follows. Hypothetical, fully-informed investors, knowing that τ_s, τ_m, τ_r, and τ_u stood at 71, 69, 31 and 69 percent (respectively) would have bid up the value of market, industrial, railroad, and utility shares by 238, 231, 102, and 230 percent (respectively). in other words, changing fundamentals in the presence of relatively constant real wages would have led investors to bid share prices up by 238, 231, 102 and 230 percent respectively. What is interesting to note is the fact that the greatest gains occurred in those sectors of the U.S. economy most likely to be affected by electrification, notably industry and, of course, utilities.

U.S. ELECTRIC POWER GENERATING CAPACITY

Admittedly, the estimates of τ, the technology shock, provided in this chapter are high. Could the U.S. economy, in general, and U.S. manufacturing in particular, have produced between 20 and 40 percent more? For example, would the supplies of available factor inputs have been sufficient? Put differently, would the supply of factor inputs throughout the 1920s not have limited growth? As was the case at the Ford Motor Company in 1913, the demand for, and not the supply of, Model Ts acted as a constraint on output. Ford's Highland Park plant, complete with its 8,000-horsepower power plant, was rated for 800,000 automobiles per annum. As we have argued, similar conditions existed throughout U.S. industry in the 1920s: electrification had increased productive capacity radically.

Was overall electricity-generating capacity in the 1920s sufficient to allow for a 30 to 40 percent increase in U.S. GNP? To answer this question, we examined the load factors in the U.S. electric power industry in the 1920s. Load was defined simply as the overall consumption of electric power, measured in kilowatt hours, to the overall installed capacity of electric power, also measured in kilowatt hours. Referring to Table 7.5, we see that throughout the 1920s, the overall electric power load factor hovered around 33 percent, which when compared to 1960 and 1970 is low. Of the 170.2 billion kilowatt hours of installed capacity in 1920, only 57.1 billion were consumed. By 1929, installed capacity had more than doubled to 339.0 billion kilowatt hours; consumption also more than doubled, to 117.9 billion kilowatt hours. The load factor, however, remained where it was in 1920. Thus, in conclusion, the supply of electric power could not and did not act as a constraint on economic growth in the 1920s.

Table 7.5
U.S. Electric Power Load Factors, 1920-1945 [*]

Year	Cap.	Cons.	Load
1920	170.2	57.1	0.33
1921	180.4	53.6	0.29
1922	186.7	61.8	0.33
1923	203.5	72.1	0.35

Table 7.5
U.S. Electric Power Load Factors, 1920-1945 (Continued)[*]

1924	227.9	40.3	0.33
1925	263.5	85.5	0.32
1926	288.5	95.1	0.32
1927	302.8	103.4	0.34
1928	322.2	109.1	0.33
1929	339.0	117.9	0.34
1930	360.5	115.7	0.32
1931	370.4	110.4	0.29
1932	375.3	100.3	0.26
1933	377.0	103.6	0.27
1934	372.2	111.5	0.29
1935	375.1	120.1	0.32
1936	381.7	137.3	0.35
1937	388.6	147.9	0.38
1938	410.6	143.3	0.34
1939	433.0	162.9	0.34
1940	446.4	181.7	0.40
1941	472.9	210.3	0.40
1942	501.3	235.4	0.46
1943	530.3	270.2	0.50
1944	550.7	275.0	0.49

[*]   Source: U.S. Department of Commerce (1975), Series S74 and S120.

COMPARISONS WITH BROOKINGS INSTITUTION ESTIMATES

In 1934, the Brookings Institution published a volume entitled *America's Capacity to Produce* in which authors Edwin G. Nourse and associates reported estimates of the U.S. economy's "ability to produce," defined as potential output from 1900 to 1929. Table 7.6, taken from this volume, shows that from 1922 to 1929, the U.S. economy repeatedly produced at levels significantly below capacity. For example, in 1922, they estimated potential productive capacity at $75.5 billion. Total income produced in 1922 was $63.4 billion, resulting in a gap of 16 percent. Throughout the 1920s, the gap stood at roughly 17 percent.

These estimates were obtained using survey data. In the early 1930s, the Brookings Institution conducted a comprehensive, economy-wide survey of U.S. productive capacity. Managers were asked to estimate potential firm output. One could argue that while such a techniques are reliable in periods of stationary technology, they may not provide accurate estimates of potential output in periods of technological change. Not having ever produced at full capacity with the new technology makes its difficult to accurately estimate maximum output. As a result, there is reason to believe that these results would be biased downward.

Table 7.6
The Brookings Institution Estimates of Potential Productive Capacity, 1922-1929 *

Year	Cap.*	Prod.*	Gap(%)
1922	75.5	63.4	16
1923	83.2	69.9	17
1924	85.1	71.5	17
1925	89.6	75.3	16
1926	91.9	77.2	16
1927	93.2	78.3	17
1928	94.9	79.7	16
1929	97.5	81.9	17

*   Source: Moulton (1935), 176.
  * Billions of constant 1929 dollars

Import Substitution: Too Little, Too Late

Having derived estimates of the output gap (actual versus potential), we now turn and examine the feasibility of import substitution (i.e. the Smoot-Hawley Tariff Bill) as a means of closing this gap. As pointed out earlier, Reed Smoot, Joseph Grundy and the Republican party were convinced that a generalized, across the board tariff hike would allow U.S. manufacturers and farmers to produce at capacity. By restricting access to the U.S. market, higher tariffs would prompt merchants to increase orders from domestic firms and in the process increase capacity utilization rates, earnings, etcetera. Again, according to Milton Merill:

> On his return to Utah in August 1932, in preparation for his final battle in political life, Smoot advised his people that it had been the common attitude in 1930 to attributed the depression to unwise governmental policies, with the Smoot-Hawley act specified. Lest there were some obsessed with heresy, he declared, "To hold the American tariff policy, or any other policy of our government, responsible for this gigantic deflationary move is only to display one's ignorance of its sweeping universal character." He found that "The world is paying for its ruthless destruction of life and property in the World War and for its failure to adjust purchasing power to productive capacity during the industrial revolution of the decade following the war." (Merrill 1990, 340)

Table 7.7 presents U.S. export and import data from 1921 to 1930. We see that from 1921 to 1929, total exports increased, as did total imports. Exports and imports of manufactures increased. Food exports decreased, while food imports increased. The U.S., however, maintained a positive balance throughout this period. The relevant question, however, is whether import substitution, in this case, the result of prohibitive tariffs, could have closed the output gap?

Table 7.7
U.S. Foreign Trade 1920-1930

	EXPT	IMPT	EXPM	IMPM	EXPF	IMPF
1921	4,379	2,509	1,627	620	685	368
1922	3,765	3,113	1,292	663	588	387

Table 7.7
U.S. Foreign Trade 1920-1930 (Continued)

1923	4,091	3,792	1,478	771	583	530
1924	4,498	3,610	1,588	749	573	522
1925	4,819	4,227	1,843	796	574	433
1926	4,712	4,431	1,957	877	503	418
1927	4,759	4,185	1,982	879	463	451
1928	5,030	4,091	2,260	906	466	406
1929	5,157	4,399	2,532	994	484	424
1930	3,781	3,061	1,898	757	363	293

With the benefit of hindsight, it is clear that even in the best of worlds (complete import substitution) tariff policy could not have closed the gap between actual and potential output. The latter was estimated at $43 billion in 1929. With total imports at $4.3 billion, complete import substitution would at best have had a marginal effect on output, employment, and more importantly, the output gap. Furthermore, with the real possibility of retaliatory tariffs on U.S. goods abroad, any increase in sales would be short lived.

In the defense of Reed Smoot and Willis C. Hawley, such estimates were unavailable in the late 1920's. The Smoot-Hawley Tariff Bill, it therefore follows, was little more than a policy heuristic, based, in large measure, on the past, specifically, on the role of tariffs in U.S. history.

Conclusions

This chapter presented estimates of τ, the rate of technological change, and potential U.S. GNP from 1925 to 1945. Together with data on actual GNP, we were able to generate estimates of the corresponding output gap. The latter ranged from 21 percent to 42 percent. These were then used to evaluate the potential efficacy of tariff policy as a means to resolve the problem of underincome. As it turned out, the output gap in all possible scenarios dwarfed U.S. imports, making for a situation in which import substitution was destined to fail, even before it began.

8

Summary and Conclusions

Q :Did the Smoot-Hawley Tariff Act make sense? A : Yes. Q : How much? A : As much as Hoover's view that the economy in 1929 was fundamentally sound, as much as attributing the Great Depression to the Stock Market Crash. As we have attempted to show here and elsewhere (Beaudreau 1996, 2004), the problem was underincome—more to the point, the inability of the U.S. economy to make the transition to the new equilibrium growth path defined by EHTCFPT. No one knew why! Not surprisingly, no one knew how to solve the problem. Only recently has the problem of underincome been studied formally, both positively and normatively.

This then begs the question, with the benefit of hindsight, did the Smoot-Hawley Tariff Act make sense? Could import substitution have closed the gap between actual and potential GNP? More specifically, could the tariffs measures contained in the Smoot-Hawley Tariff Bill of 1929 have closed an output gap estimated at between 16 to 43 percent? The answer is no. Ironically, after a century of policies aimed at closing the economy to world trade, the Republican party felt that it was necessary to go to the proverbial well once more. Unfortunately, the well was dry. As pointed out in the last chapter, a complete interdiction on imports would not have sufficed, would not have closed the chasm that separated actual and potential output.

How then should Reed Smoot, Willis C. Hawley, and the Republican party be judged? As zealots? As shortsighted? As insular? As xenophobic?

I would argue that neither of these labels is accurate and, more importantly, appropriate. As we pointed out in earlier work, the problem of underincome is as old as industrialization, dating back to early 19th-century Great Britain. By

157

the 1930s, with the exception of a handful of scholars, five generations of Anglo-Saxon economists had failed to grasp the subtleties of paradigm technological change-based transitions from one equilibrium growth path to another. Reed Smoot and the Republican party we argue played their best hand, which, unfortunately, didn't amount to much—a pair of fives, at best! As evidenced by his declarations both before and after final passage, Smoot was painfully aware of the failure of income and expenditure to keep up with output. Unfortunately, he, his Senate colleagues, his Republican colleagues, and the economics profession as a whole did not know why? Enter the heuristics that were the Smoot-Hawley Tariff Bill of 1929 and the National Industrial Recovery Act of 1933. Both are in dire need of being rehabilitated.

With the benefit of hindsight, the Smoot-Hawley Tariff Act of 1930 and the National Industrial Recovery Act of 1933 marked a watershed of sorts, a continental divide between two approaches to the problem of "making the market." Until the early 20th century, the United States had sold on world markets without however "making them." All of this changed in the 1910s and 1920s, with EHTCFPT's. Figurately speaking, the U.S. had become a colossus, the likes of which the world had never seen. Potential wealth reached epic proportions. The problem, however, lay in realizing this potential.

APPENDIX A

Chronology of the Events Leading up to the Stock Market Crashes

Here, a day-to-day account of the demise of the Hoover administration's tariff initiative is provided, along with analysis of its impact on stock market prices from Monday, October 21, 1929 to Wednesday, October 30, 1929. As was argued in Chapter 4, and as will become more apparent here, the two major stock market crashes that occurred in this ten-day interval were the direct result of tariff-related "bad news."

The first stock market crash lasted two trading days: Wednesday, October 23, 1929, and Thursday, October 24, 1930. The *Dow Jones Industrials Average* lost a total of 27 points on an initial value of 326.51 (October 22, 1929). From Monday, October 21 through to Wednesday, October 23 (inclusive), the debate on the Smoot-Hawley Tariff Bill came to a head. For example, on Monday, October 21, the headlines of the *New York Times* read "Watson Asks Speed on Tariff As Vital to Stable Business." Senator James E. Watson of Indiana, Republican leader of the Senate, "said that the business man was hesitating to make heavy commitments until economic conditions were stabilized by a new tariff law."[1] In fact, Watson attributed the developments on Wall Street (i.e. price weakness) to the plight of the tariff bill: "He saw in the New York stock market break at the end of the week one reaction that might be charged to Senate inability to hasten the passage of the bill."[2]

On the following day, Tuesday, October 22, 1929, the first piece of tariff-related "bad news" occurred. The headlines of *The New York Times* read: "Senate Firmly Bars Farm Tariff Limit." By a vote of 64 to 10, the Senate defeated the Thomas Recommittal Plan, an amendment that sought to limit tariff revisions to duties on farm products. The "bad news," however, was the reported "shift in focus of the Democratic-Progressive Republican coalition." Specifically, "Just before the vote, Senator Simmons, ranking minority member of the *Finance Committee*, revealed that Democrats at least want the rates on industrial articles kept before the Senate because they wish to reduce not only the duties recommended by the committee, but those in the existing Fordney-McCumber Tariff law."[3] Clearly, the tide had shifted: not only would tariffs on manufactures not rise, in all likelihood, they would fall. Consequently, U.S. firms' domestic sales, market share and earnings would fall, not rise.

Making matters worse was the fact that on Monday, October 21, 1929, the Senate committee investigating the activities of lobbyists learned that secrets on the tariff bill had been leaked to *The Connecticut Manufactures Association*. The headline on the following day (Tuesday October 22, 1929), read: "Note Hints Secrets on Tariff Bill Got to Manufacturers." The *New York Times* reported: "A memorandum in the office of *The Connecticut Manufacturers Association* which, according to Senator Walsh of Montana, suggested that information had been obtained on secret debates in the *Senate Finance Committee* on the tariff bill, figured in evidence today before the Senate committee investigating the activities of lobbyists."[4]

The following day, October 22, 1929, the Democratic-Insurgent Republican coalition, fresh from its victory on the Thomas Recommittal Plan, set its sights on lowering tariffs on manufactures and forced cuts in chemical rates, as reported on the front page of the *New York Times* on Wednesday, October 23, 1929.

> Aided by four Old-Guard Republicans, the Democratic-Progressive coalition won the first test vote on the rates of the Smoot-Hawley tariff bill when taken up in the Senate today. The count was 45 in favor and 33 against. The item on which the vote was taken was incidental, but the result served to show that the coalition was nearly intact in its initial drive and also that it still held control in the Senate.[5]

By then, it was clear that the administration had lost control of the tariff initiative. The business community's worst-case scenario (i.e. the *status quo*) got even worse. Not only would rates on manufactures fail to rise, everything pointed to tariff reductions. Stock prices crashed on Wednesday, October 23, 1929, and Thursday, October 24, 1929. By Friday, October 25, 1929, the market had lost 27 points, which corresponds to 8.28 percent of its initial value.

As it turned out, this was only the beginning. By Thursday, October 24, 1929, it was clear that the administration's tariff initiative had back-fired. Not only would tariffs on manufactures fail to rise, all signs indicated that they would fall. The tide had clearly shifted. This prompted a number of angry responses. On October 24, Joseph R. Grundy, president of *The Pennsylvania Manufacturers Association* and one of the main architects of Hoover's Kansas City Platform, renewed calls for higher tariffs on manufactures, pointing out (correctly) that 23 million people had supported the protective principle (i.e. in the 1928 presidential election). *The New York Times* headlines on October 25, 1929, read: "Grundy Says Lobby Is Needed to Uphold Party Tariff Vows." Testifying before the Senate Lobbying Investigating Committee, Grundy, president of *The Pennsylvania Manufactures Association*, lashed out against the opponents of the tariff bill.

> Joseph R. Grundy, head of the Pennsylvania Manufacturers Association and a conspicuous figure for years in the Republican organization of that State, told the Senate Lobby Investigating Committee today that the rates in the pending tariff bill had been adopted in accordance with pledges in the Kansas City platform upon which President Herbert C. Hoover made his successful run at the Presidency. The witness declared that 23,000,000 voters had endorsed the protective principle, and that if consumers had wanted lower tariff duties they would have shown it by electing Alfred E. Smith to the Presidency.[6]

Surprisingly, throughout this "critical" period, President Herbert C. Hoover, remained mute on the tariff question. Some disillusioned ranking Senate Republicans declared the tariff bill dead. On Saturday, October 26, 1929, Republican Senator Reed went on the record in Philadelphia predicting that the tariff bill would "die in the present session." On Sunday, October 27, 1929, Senators Smoot and Borah, opponents on the tariff issue, contradicted Senator Reed. The headlines of *The New York Times* of Monday, October 28, 1928 summarized the weekend tryst as follows: "Leaders Insist Tariff Will Pass: Smoot and Borah Contradict Reed, Who Told Philadelphians Bill Was Dead."

White the fate of the tariff bill admittedly is in doubt in the minds of many of the Senators now trying to agree on a measure that will be passed and meet the approval of the President, a statement made by Senator Reed of Pennsylvania in a Philadelphia address last night that the bill would die in the present session came as a great surprise to Republican and Democratic leaders here. Senator Smoot, Republican of Utah, took direct issue with Senator Reed and, although agreeing that chances of the bill passing in the special session were dim, predicted that it would be acted on in the regular session opening in December. "If that is Senator Reed's opinion", said Mr. Smoot, "I suppose he has a right to express it. But it isn't the view of the Finance Committee. If they take as much time debating it as they have been taking, it will not pass in the session, but it will go on to the next session." Apparently, this remark was based on the fact that the tariff bill, as it is being rewritten by the Republican-Democratic coalition, bears little resemblance to the bill which Old-Guard Republicans want adopted.[7]

In hindsight, this event was the proverbial straw that broke the camel's back. It was now painfully clear to investors and businessmen alike that the bill was dead. The stock market reacted, losing 38 points on Monday, October 28, 1929, on an initial value of 298.97 (October 26, 1929). With stock prices tumbling, Republican Senator Hiram W. Johnson of California and Democratic Senator Pat Harrison of Mississippi called on President Herbert C. Hoover for guidance on the tariff issue. *The New York Times* headlines on Tuesday, October 29, 1929, read: "Senators renew Demand On Hoover For Tariff Stand."

During a debate amply illustrating the nervousness of the Senate over the ultimate fate of the Smoot-Hawley tariff bill today, President Hoover was again called upon to solve the situation by declaring his position on agricultural and industrial products. The demand, made by Senators Johnson, Republican of California, and Harrison, Democrat of Mississippi, was injected when Senator Johnson sought definite information on Senator Reed's Saturday night statement in Philadelphia that the bill was dead.[8]

Hoover maintained his silence. The following day, Tuesday October 29, the market plunged for a second time, losing another 30 points, or 12 percent of its value. Tariff-related "bad news" continued to literally pour out of Washington after the crashes. By Tuesday, October 29, 1929, the Old-Guard Republicans were prepared to let the tariff bill die in session (Clearly, existing tariffs on manufactures were preferred to the proposed lower tariffs). The

Democratic-Insurgent Republican coalition, however, was determined to drive the bill, as amended, through the Senate. *The New York Times* of Wednesday, October 30, 1929 ran the following headline: "Coalition Fighting Move To Kill Tariff."

> Faced by Old-Guard Republican willingness to leave the Smoot-Hawley tariff bill to its fate, the Democratic Progressive Republican coalition was today more determined than ever to drive the bill through the Senate and force the conservatives to accept it in a completely rewritten form. Coalition strategy was centered upon fixing on the Old Guard leaders any responsibility for abandonment of the remodeled bill with the Simmons-Norris flexible amendment to the farm debenture plan. To those old-line Republicans who are now ready to desert the measure, the coalition applied the unflattering comparison of rats and a sinking ship.[9]

Sharing the headlines on October 30, 1929 was Joseph R. Grundy, President of the Pennsylvania Manufacturers Association. *The New York Times* headlines read: "Grundy for Curbing Backward States on the Tariff Bill." The subtitles read: "Veteran Republican Lobbyist Tells Senate Inquiry the West Needs Silencing," "Pennsylvania Knows Best," "Unfortunate, He Holds, That the Constitution Gives Equal Votes to States in Senate," and "Battles Investigators." By this point in time, there was no longer any doubt in investors minds: the original Smoot-Hawley Tariff Bill was dead. Manufacturers would not reap the benefits of higher tariffs.

APPENDIX B

The National Industrial Recovery Act of 1933

Congressional Record. June 16,1933 (H.R. 5155)

AN ACT
To encourage national industrial recovery, to foster fair competition, and to provide for the construction of certain useful public works, and for other purposes.
Be it enacted by the Senate and House of Representatives of the United States of America in Congress assembled.

TITLE 1—INDUSTRIAL RECOVERY
Section 1. A national emergency productive of widespread unemployment and disorganization of industry, which burdens interstate and foreign commerce, affects the public welfare, and undermines the standards of living of the American people, is hereby declared to exist. It is hereby declared to be the policy of Congress to remove obstructions to the free flow of interstate and foreign commerce which tend to diminish the amount thereof; and to provide for the general welfare by promoting the organization of industry for the purpose of cooperative action among trade groups, to induce and maintain united action of labor and management under adequate governmental sanctions and supervision, to eliminate unfair competitive practices, to promote the fullest possible utilization of the present productive capacity of industries, to avoid undue restriction of production (except as may be temporarily required), to

increase the consumption of industrial and agricultural products by increasing purchasing power, to reduce and relieve unemployment, to improve standards of labor, and otherwise to rehabilitate industry and to conserve natural resources.

ADMINISTRATIVE AGENCIES

Sec. 2. (a) To effectuate the policy of this title, the President is hereby authorized to establish such agencies, to accept and utilize such voluntary and uncompensated services, to appoint, without regard to the provisions of the civil service laws, such officers and employees, and to utilize such Federal officers and employees, and, with the consent of the State, such State and local officers and employees, as they may find necessary, to prescribe their authorities, duties, responsibilities, and tenure, and, without regard to the Classification Act of 1923, as amended, to fix the compensation of any officers, and employees so appointed.

(b) The President may delegate any of his functions and powers under this title to such officers, agents, and employees as he may designate or appoint, and may establish an industrial planning and research agency to aid in carrying out his functions under this title.

(c) This title shall cease to be in effect and any agencies established hereunder shall cease to exist at the expiration of two years after the date of enactment of this Act, or sooner if the President shall by proclamation or the Congress shall by joint resolution declare that the emergency recognized by section 1 has ended.

CODES OF FAIR COMPETITION

Sec. 3 (a) Upon the application to the President by one or more trade or industrial associations or groups, the President may approve a code or codes of fair competition for the trade or industry or subdivision thereof, represented by the applicant or applicants, if the President finds (1) that such associations or groups impose no inequitable restrictions on admission to membership therein and are truly representative of such trades or industries or subdivisions thereof, and (2) that such code or codes are not designed to promote monopolies or to eliminate or oppress small enterprises and will not operate to discriminate against them, and will tend to effectuate the policy of this title: Provided, That such code or codes shall not permit monopolies or monopolistic practices: Provided further, That where such code affects or codes affect the services and welfare of persons engaged in other steps of the economic process, nothing in this section shall deprive such persons of the right to be heard prior to approval by the President of such code or codes. The President may, as a condition of his approval of any such code, impose such conditions (including requirements for the making of reports and the keeping of accounts) for the protection of consumers, competitors, employees, and others, and in furtherance of the public interest, and may provide such exceptions to and exemptions from the provisions of such codes, as the President in his discretion deems necessary to effectuate the policy herein declared.

(b) After the President shall have approved any such code, the provisions of such code shall be the standards of fair competition for such trade or industry or subdivision thereof. Any violation of such standards in any transaction in or affecting interstate or foreign commerce shall be deemed an unfair method of competition in commerce within the meaning of the Federal Trade Commission Act, as amended; but nothing in this title shall be construed to impair the powers of the Federal Trade Commission under such Act, as amended.

(c) The several district courts of the United States are hereby invested with Jurisdiction to prevent and restrain violations of any code of fair competition approved under this title; and it shall be the duty of the several district attorneys of the United States, in their respective districts, under the direction of the Attorney General, to institute proceedings in equity to prevent and restrain such violations.

(d) Upon his own motion, or if complaint is made to the President that abuses inimical to the public interest and contrary to the policy herein declared are prevalent in any trade or industry or subdivision thereof, and if no code of fair competition therefore has theretofore been approved by the President, the President, after such public notice and hearing as he shall specify, may prescribe and approve a code of fair competition for such trade or industry or subdivision thereof, which shall have the same effect as a code of fair competition approved by the President under subsection (a) of this section

(e) On his own motion, or if any labor organization, or any trade or industrial organization, association, or group, which has complied with the provisions of this title, shall make complaint to the President that any article or articles are being imported into the United States in substantial quantities or increasing ratio to domestic production of any competitive article or articles and on such terms or under such conditions as to render ineffective or seriously to endanger the maintenance of any code or agreement under this title, the President may cause an immediate investigation to be made by the United States Tariff

Commission, which shall give precedence to investigations under this subsection, and if, after such investigation and such public notice and hearing as he shall specify, the President shall find the existence of such facts, he shall, in order to effectuate the policy of this title, direct that the article or articles concerned shall be permitted entry into the United States only upon such terms and conditions and subject to the payment of such fees and to such limitations in the total quantity which may be imported (in the course of any specified period or periods) as he shall find it necessary to prescribe in order that the entry thereof shall not render or tend to render ineffective any code or agreement made under this title. in order to enforce any limitations imposed on the total quantity of imports, in any specified period or periods, of any article or articles under this subsection, the President may forbid the importation of such article or articles unless the importer shall have first obtained from the Secretary of the Treasury a license pursuant to such regulations as the President may prescribe. Upon information of any action by the President under this subsection the Secretary of the Treasury shall, through the proper officers, permit entry of the article or articles specified only upon such terms and conditions and subject to such fees, to such limitations in the quantity which may be imported, and to such requirements of license, as the President shall have directed. The decision of the President as to facts shall be conclusive. Any condition or limitation of entry under this subsection shall continue in effect until the President shall find and inform the Secretary of the Treasury that the conditions which led to the imposition of such condition or limitation upon entry no longer exists.

(f) When a code of fair competition has been approved or prescribed by the President under this title, any violation of any provision thereof in any transaction in or affecting interstate or foreign commerce shall be a misdemeanor and upon conviction thereof an offender shall be fined not more than $500 for each offense, and each day such violation continues shall be deemed a separate offense.

AGREEMENTS AND LICENSES

Sec. 4. (a) The President is authorized to enter into agreements with, and to approve voluntary agreements between and among, persons engaged in a trade or industry, labor organizations, and trade or industrial organizations, associations, or groups, relating to any trade or industry, if in his judgment such agreements will aid in effectuating the policy of this title with respect to transactions in or affecting interstate or foreign commerce, and will be consistent with the requirements of clause (2) of subsection (a) of section 3 for a code of fair competition.

(b) Whenever the President shall find that destructive wage or price cutting or other activities contrary to the policy of this title are being practiced in any trade or industry or any subdivision thereof, and, after such public notice and hearing as he shall specify, shall find it essential to license business enterprises in order to make effective a code of fair competition or an agreement under this title or otherwise to effectuate the policy of this title, and shall publicly so announce, no person shall, after a date fixed in such announcement, engage in or carry any business, in or affecting interstate or foreign commerce, specified in such announcement, unless he shall have first obtained a license issued pursuant to such regulations as the President shall prescribe. The President may suspend or revoke any such license, after due notice and opportunity for hearing, for violations of the terms or conditions thereof. Any order of the President suspending or revoking any such license shall be final if in accordance with law. Any person who, without such a license or in violation of any condition thereof, carries on any such business for which a license is so required, shall, upon conviction thereof, be fined not more than $500, or imprisoned not more than six months or both, and each day such violation continues shall be deemed a separate offense. Notwithstanding the provisions of section 2 (c), this subsection shall cease to be in effect at the expiration of one year after the date of enactment of this Act or sooner if the President shall by proclamation or the Congress shall by joint resolution declare that the emergency recognized by section 1 has ended.

Sec. 5. White this title is in effect (or the case of a license, while section 4 (a) is in effect) and for sixty days thereafter, any code, agreement, or license approved, prescribed, or issued and in effect under this title, and any action complying with the provisions thereof taken during such period, shall be exempt from the provisions of the antitrust laws of the United States. Nothing in this Act, and no regulation there under, shall prevent an individual from pursuing the vocation of manual labor and selling or trading the products thereof; nor shall anything in this Act, or regulation there under, prevent anyone from marketing or trading the produce of his farm.

LIMITATIONS UPON APPLICATION OF TITLE

Sec, 6. (a) No trade or industrial association or group shall be eligible to receive the benefit of the provisions of this title until it files with the President a statement containing such information relating to the activities of the association or group as the President shall by regulation prescribe.

(b) The President is authorized to prescribe rules and regulations designed to insure that any organization availing itself of the benefits of this shall be truly representative of the trade or industry or subdivision thereof represented by such organization. Any organization violating any such rule or regulation shall cease to be entitled to the benefits of this title.

(c) Upon the request of the President, the Federal Trade Commission shall make such investigations as may be necessary to enable the President to carry out the provisions of this title, and for such purposes the Commission shall have all the powers vested in it with respect of investigations under the Federal Trade Commission Act, as amended.

Sec. 7. (a) Every code of fair competition, agreement, and license approved, prescribed, or issued under this title shall contain the following conditions: (1) That employees shall have the right to organize and bargain collectively through representatives of their own choosing, and shall be free from the interference, restraint, or coercion of employers of labor, or their agents, in the designation of such representatives or in self-organization or in other concerted activities for the purpose of collective bargaining or other mutual aid or protection; (2) that no employee and no one seeking employment shall be required as a condition of employment to join any company union or to refrain from joining, organizing, or assisting a labor organization of his own choosing; and (3) that employers shall comply with the maximum hours of labor, minimum rates of pay, and other conditions of employment, approved or prescribed by the President.

(b) The President shall, so far as practicable, afford every opportunity to employers and employees in any trade or industry of subdivision thereof with respect to which the conditions referred to in clauses (1) and (2) of subsection (a) prevail, to establish by mutual agreement, the standards as to the maximum hours of labor, minimum rates of pay, and such other conditions of employment as may be necessary in such trade or industry or subdivision thereof to effectuate the policy of this title; and the standards established in such agreements, when approved by the President, shall have the same effect as a code of fair competition, approved by the President under subsection (a) of section 3.

(c) Where no such mutual agreement has been approved by the President he may investigate the labor practices, policies, wages, hours of labor, and conditions of employment in such trade or industry or subdivision thereof; and upon the basis of such investigations, and after such hearings as the President finds advisable, he is authorized to prescribe a limited code of fair competition fixing such maximum hours of labor, minimum rates of pay, and other conditions of employment in the trade or industry or subdivision thereof investigated as he finds to be necessary to effectuate the policy of this title, which shall have the same effect as a code of fair competition approved by the President under subsection (a) of section 3. The President may differentiate according to experience and skill of the employees affected and according to the locality of employment; but no attempts shall be made to introduce any classification according to the nature of the work involved which might tend to set a maximum as well as a minimum wage.

(d) As used in this title, the term "person" includes any individual, partnership, association, trust, or corporation; and the terms "interstate and foreign commerce" and "interstate or foreign commerce" include, except where otherwise indicated, trade or commerce among the several States and with foreign nations, or between the District of Columbia or any Territory of the United States and any State, Territory, or foreign nation, or between any insular possessions or other place under the jurisdiction of the United States or the District of Columbia or any foreign nation or with the District of Columbia or any Territory or any insular possession or other place under the jurisdiction of the United States.

Endnotes

Chapter 2

1. Among the shortcomings of this literature is the presumption that specialization is independent of markets (exchange technology). Put differently, the decision to specialize (as opposed to remaining autarkic) is viewed as independent of the relevant exchange technology. Clearly, a more reasonable approach would be to model the problem simultaneously. That is, agents would decide to specialize or not, based on the exchange technology in place, and the exchange technology in place would depend on whether agents specialized

2. See Silver (1994) for evidence of non-governmental media of exchange.

3. Where markets replace government hierarchy, merchants may be former functionaries.

4. One could argue that in the absence of the desire on the part of Homo-sapiens-sapiens to dominate others (empire-build), the world today would be quite different, to say the least.

5. By spontaneous trade, it should be understood trade between individual agents.

6. One could go as far as arguing that public choice-related trade and civilization are synonymous, civilization being defined as urban-rural specialization dominated by centralized government (administration and defense) and religion. See Dudley (1991) for more.

7. It could be argued that trade, both in the 19th and 20th centuries, was an amalgam of forced and spontaneous, with the latter increasing more rapidly than the former.

8. Such was the underlying theme of Adam Smith's "Wealth of Nations."

9. One could argue that the merchant's problem is no different from the producer's problem (services). Merchants add value to goods/services not unlike any producer in the value added chain. To do so, however, is to ignore the special place merchants play, individually and collectively, in western industrialized (read: market) economies. First, the merchant is the last link between consumers and producers. Second, the merchant, unlike an up-stream or downstream producer, deals with thousands if not millions of customers. Third, the merchant's demand for goods and services is determined not by downstream producers, but by all producers, via their factor market behavior).

10. In early civilizations, governments issued money (currency). This function, however, was, with the founding of the Bank of England in 1645, transferred to the private sector. Nonetheless, the government—in this case, the...—still exercised control over the supply of money. A good example of this is the Bank Charter Act of 1843, which saw limits imposed on the amount of credit the Bank of England could issue.

11. One could assume the existence of numerous merchants, without affecting any of the results. we shall return to this later.

12. For the sake of simplicity, we ignore, to begin with, energy and all organizational inputs other than capital and labor (Beaudreau 1998,1999). This is motivated, in large part, by exchange-related concerns, namely the preponderance of labor and capital costs in overall costs (i.e. of value added).

13. This mimics the short-run production analysis found in standard neoclassical production theory (fixed price).

14. This is consistent with the observed practice of remitting profits once revenues are received, and outstanding debts have been paid. Unlike all other costs, profits are a residual form of factor payment.

15. Clearly, this is a simplifying assumption, having no effect whatsoever on the outcome.

16. Given the heterogeneity of agents (producers and merchants, these states of nature should be seen as averages, describing central tendency. Clearly, not all merchants and not all producers think and reason alike.

17. This, we argue, explains why large banks typically have an economics department whose chief role is forecasting. Specifically, as banks have a double stake in output, via the producer and the merchant, they stand to lose the most.

18. we implicitly assume that the economy is growing at a rate n, where n is the rate of growth of the labor force.

19. Another way of looking at this is in terms of public goods. By raising wages (τ percent), producer ic creates a public good in the form of money income. Assuming that workers consume all n goods, it follows that all other consumption goods producers will benefit by way of higher sales.

20. Specifically, they would capture $\tau[Vc + Vk]$.

21. Paul Sweezy examined a similar question in his 1939 article entitled "Demand under Conditions of Oligopoly."

22. Perhaps this explains the asymmetry one typically finds in trade negotiations, where countries promote their exports, but fail to promote foreign imports, thus depriving their citizens of the much-anticipated gains from trade.

23. Alternatively, financial corporations could come into being, buying and selling foreign debt.

Chapter 3

1. See Rosenberg and Birdzell (1986).

2. Ford was to maintain a lifelong friendship with Thomas Edison, the father of direct current (DC) and a pioneer in the electrification of American life. To pay tribute to Edison, he created the Edison Institute on the grounds of the Henry Ford Museum, in Dearborn, Michigan.

3. For a detailed account of the genesis of the automated assembly line at the Ford Motor Company, see David Hounshell (1984), especially Ch. 6.

4. This is consistent with historian David A. Hounshell's view of Ford's contribution to mass production. According to him:

    In less than a decade, the Ford Motor Company brought together the best of the armory practice with the rapidly developing techniques of pressed steel work. To these approaches, Ford production men added fresh thinking about work sequences, tool design, and controlling the pace of work in the Ford factory. When challenged to produce more of the standardized Model T's at lower cost and when allowed virtually free reign to experiment with new methods, the Ford team brought a revolution in manufacturing: mass production. The development of the moving assembly line was the key element in this revolution. (Hounshell 1984, 329)

5. Electric power continued to be the lifeline of the manufacturing process at the Ford Motor Company's Rouge River plant which was built in the late 1910s through early 1920s. According to Hounshell (1984, 268), a 30,000 kilowatt power plant provided electricity to both the Rouge plant and the Highland Park plant.

6. According to David A. Hounshell, the Highland Park power plant was as much a source of pride for Henry Ford as the assembly tine.

7. Daniel Raff and Lawrence Summers, in a 1987 article entitled "Did Henry Ford Pay Efficiency Wages?" argue that the five-dollar day was an attempt by Henry Ford to stem absenteeism, reduce turnover, and raise productivity. There is no doubt that these factors played a role in his decision, as evidenced by statements made by Ford himself afterward (although it could be argued that these statements were an attempt on the part of Ford to deflect criticism). The problem with this argument, however, lies with the magnitude of the wage increase. The theory of efficiency wages holds that by raising wages above the industry average, firms can de facto force workers to be more productive. Nowhere is it mentioned that wages have to double. One is left wondering whether Henry Ford could not have reduced absenteeism, lowered worker turnover, and raised productivity, by simply raising wages by as little as 10 percent?

8. See Chapter 8 for more on the choice of the relevant base year.

9. New York Times, February 15, 1929.

10. One could argue that the very nature of high-throughput, continuous-flow mass production techniques, namely not being embodied-in-capital, explains its obscurity in the literature. Compared to the first industrial revolution which saw the introduction of machinery per se, the electrification of U.S. industry went relatively unnoticed.

11. In an article entitled 'The Minimum Wage and Efficiency," which appeared in the September 1923 issue of the American Economic Review, Filene argued that the minimum wage would eliminate the waste (i.e. unused capacity) that characterized U.S. business at the time.

To those who are against the minimum wage law, the easiest solution to their business problem seems to be to cut wages down. But they do not see what is really the big cost of business-waste, and devote themselves to getting rid of that. Mr. Hoover and his group of engineers have made a report on waste in industry which compared with what 1 am saying here in the subject is very mild. When we are forced by the existence of a minimum wage to apply our corrective endeavors to the real source of high costs-waste-we shall be taking a real step forward. (1923, 415)

12. Edward A. Filene's two books should be seen as outgrowths of his 1923 *American Economic Review* article entitled "The Minimum Wage and Efficiency." For example, in concluding his case for a minimum wage, he cited the ease of Henry Ford and the Ford Motor Company:

In this connection, we will call attention to a result which cannot be ignored to the man who has produced the best commodity for the price of its kind in the world, produced it in quantities never before dreamed of, and produced it so cheap that it can be sold in competition with the cheap labor of Europe-so cheap, indeed, that no country can make it to compete with him. I refer to Henry Ford. He has produced twelve hundred thousand automobiles a year-eight a minute-has financed his whole business from the profits, and has become the richest man in the world. And the minimum wage he pays is so high that if it were proposed in Massachusetts those who advocated it would be set down as crazy. Even at his high minimum wage he has been able to employ the lame, the crippled, and the blind of the community, not as a charity, but at a profit. The statistics in his autobiography covering these facts are amazing. The demonstration of the possibility of the minimum wage speaks louder than my words, and I hope it may be borne in mind that any decision of the minimum wage question. (1923,415)

13. In *Captains of Consciousness*, Stuart Ewen points out that in the early-to-mid 1920s, the industrial vanguard of the business community saw the need to "endow the masses with what historian Norma Ware has called the money, commodity and psychic wages correlative and responsive to the route of industrial capitalism. There was a dramatic movement toward conditions which would make mass consumption feasible: higher wages and shorter hours" (1976, 29).

Chapter 4

1. While Republicans argued that the economy was sound, Senator Robert F. Wagner maintained that unemployment was on the rise. As it turns out, because the U.S. government did not collect detailed data on unemployment, the ensuing debate was based more on anecdotal evidence than on hard facts.

2. *New York Times*, March 8, 1928.

3. *Congressional Record*, March 7, 1928, 4231.

4. The 1928 Republican convention was held from June 12 to 15 at the Civic Auditorium in Kansas City, Missouri.

5. The 1928 Democratic convention was held from June 26 to 29 at the Sam Houston Hall, in Houston, Texas.

6. This view of the role of tariff policy in the 1928 presidential campaign contrasts with that of Frank Taussig who in the February 1930 edition of *The Quarterly Journal of Economics* wrote:

We come, then, to the tariff debates and votes of the special session of 1929. A special session of Congress was called by President Hoover for June 1929; but it was to deal primarily with the agricultural situation. As regards the tariff, conditions were quite different from those of 1922.

There was no industrial depression in 1928, no general panic about dumping and the floods of cheap imports. in the presidential campaign the tariff question played no part. (1930, 180)

7. *New York Times,* July 29, 1929.

8. According to Harold U. Faulkner, the Kansas City convention was under the control of "the Hoover contingent and the industrial interests of the Northeast" (1950, 306).

9. Why Senator Reed Smoot from Utah, a predominantly agricultural state in the 1920s, became the chief advocate for higher tariffs on manufactures is open for debate. Was it power politics? Was it party politics? Was it the fact that he was involved in the woolen-goods industry? Clearly, his constituents, like those of neighboring California, had the most to lose from high-priced manufactures. Was he playing power politics with East-Coast Old-Guard Republicans such as Joseph R. Grundy of Philadelphia? These questions require further study.

10. Philadelphia, it would appear, was a tariff stronghold in the early twentieth century and the seat of pro-tariff forces in the United States. For example, the Wharton Business School at the University of Pennsylvania was established in 1881 by Joseph Wharton, who insisted that all students be ingrained with the fundamental truth of tariff protection.

11. For more on this, see the *New York Times,* February 10, 1929.

12. *New York Times,* May 9, 1929.

13. *New York Times,* September 6, 1929.

14. Vulcain prophetically anticipated the first two policy responses to over-production, namely, higher tariffs (i.e. the Smoot-Hawley Tariff Bill of 1929) and higher wages (i.e. the National Industrial Recovery Act of 1933).

15. *New York Times,* January 24, 1928.

CHAPTER 5

1. It could be argued that the plight of the farmer in the 1920s was also largely the result of developments at the Ford Motor Company in the 1910s. The Model T revolutionized transportation in America, not to mention the world, as horses, mules and oxen were replaced by internal-combustion engines as the principal power source. Consequently, the demand for horse feed (e.g. hay, oats, and barley) fell dramatically, resulting in a drop in the price of cereals. Put differently, agriculture was a victim of the transportation revolution that was in full swing in the 1920s and 1930s.

2. *The New York Times*, July 4, 1929.

3. *The New York Times*, July 4, 1929.

4. *The New York Times*, July 8, 1929.

5. *The New York Times*, August 23, 1929.

6. Judging from President Hoover's position throughout the debate, it is clear that the tariff issue (i.e. higher tariffs) was more a party issue (especially with the Old-Guard) than a reflection of the president's personal views. Interestingly enough, throughout his first year in the Oval Office, Hoover, the first Technocratic president, did, at times, refer to the need for firms to increase wages. For more on Technocracy, which recognized the importance of energy in the economy and in society, see Scott *et al.* (1933). Thus, it could be argued that, at least conceptually, Hoover shared the principal objectives of Franklin D. Roosevelt's National Industrial Recovery Act of 1933.

7. *The New York Times*, September 7, 1929.

8. By administration, it should be understood the "Old-Guard Republicans" who controlled the party.

9. *The New York Times*, October 17, 1929.

10. *The New York Times*, October 17, 1929.

11. A third piece of bad news was a report that secret details on the tariff bill had been leaked to manufacturers. According to the October 23, 1929 edition of *The New York Times,* the Senate Committee investigating the activities of lobbyists heard testimony that the Connecticut Manufacturer's Association had obtained information on secret debates in the Senate Finance Committee.

12. *The New York Times,* October 22, 1929.

13. *The New York Times,* October 23, 1929.

14. In *The Way the World Works: How Economies Fail and Succeed,* author Jude Wanniski makes the reverse argument. The stock market crash, he argues, was caused by the increasing likelihood that the Smoot-Hawley Tariff Bill would pass. He bases his case on the fact that on October 21, 1929, the Senate rejected efforts by the Finance Committee to limit the tariff increases to agriculture which he incorrectly interprets as a vote of confidence for across-the-board tariff hikes on manufactures. The vote in question was on a motion by Senator John W. Thomas of Oklahoma to limit tariff revision to duties on farm products [*The New York Times,* October 22, 1929]. The coalition of Democrats and Insurgent Republicans which controlled the Senate, wanted to reduce rates on industrial articles and voted against this motion, which would have maintained tariff rates on manufactures at levels specified by the Fordney-McCumber Tariff Act. Thus, this should be seen as a step back for Senators Smoot and Borah, as well as President Hoover, who favored higher tariffs on industrial articles, and not a step forward, as Wanniski maintains.

15. *The New York Times,* October 28, 1929.

16. Of particular interest is the fact that on both days, October 25, 1929 and October 30, 1929, "bad" tariff news shared the headlines of the *New York Times.* On October 25, 1929, the headlines read: "Grundy Says Lobby Is Needed to Uphold Party Tariff Vows" and "Worst Stock Crash Stemmed by Banks; 12,894,650-Share Day Swamps Market; Leaders Confer, Find Conditions Sound." On October 30, 1929, the headlines read "Grundy for Curbing Backward States on the Tariff Bill" and "Stocks Collapse in 16,410,030-Share Day, But Rally At Close Cheers Brokers"; Bankers Optimistic, To Continue Aid." Furthermore, on October 23, 1929, the

headlines read: "Prices of Stocks Crash in Heavy Liquidation, Total Drop of Billions" and "Coalition Breaks Over Carbide Rate" (see Appendix A).

17. *The New York Times,* October 24,1929.

18. *The New York Times,* December 23, 1929.

19. Among the more prominent Insurgent Republicans, one finds Senator George Norris of Nebraska and Senator Thomas D. Schall of Minnesota.

20. The stock market responded negatively. The Dow Jones industrial average fell 56 points from June 1, 1930 to June 18,1930 on an initial value of 274.45. This stands in stark contrast to the stock market's initial response to the Hoover administration's tariff initiative. This can be attributed to a number of factors. For example, in 1928, investors naively believed that the promised tariff hikes would not prompt retaliatory measures aimed at U.S. exports on the part of its trading partners. The events of the summer of 1929 and the spring of 1930 changed this: France and Germany promised retaliatory tariff measures aimed at U.S. exports. The United States had come of age. A minor figure in the late eighteenth century and nineteenth century, the United States had become an important economic force in the world economy in the late 1920s.

21. It is my view that in—the absence of the Smoot-Hawley Tariff Bill, the U.S. economy would have spontaneously lapsed into an equally severe depression owing to the widening gap between production and consumption. Specifically, it seems likely that the continued diffusion of the techniques of mass production and the resulting increase in productive capacity could, at any time, have led to a sudden and sharp decrease in investment expenditure.

22. One could argue that the fall in aggregate expenditure in the early 1930s prompted firms to "electrify" as a means of reducing variable (i.e. labor) costs. Lower sales and revenues squeezed profit margins; continuous-flow production techniques provided firms with a respite. .

23. *The New York Times,* October 17,1929.

24. *The New York Times,* October 21, 1929.

25. *The New York Times,* February 9, 1926.

26. *The New York Times,* June 11, 1930.

CHAPTER 6

1. See Appendix B.

2. The NIRA, as it relates to monopoly and combines behavior in general, is more complex than most writers have argued. The purpose of the NIRA was to foster macroeconomic cooperation, while encouraging microeconomic competition. For example, in Section I, there are multiple references to entry at the industry level and the importance accorded to it in legislation. Thus, it is unfair to charge that the NIRA was an attempt at cartelizing the economy.

3. According to biographer Michael Namorato, Rexford G. Tugwell's interest in technology and technological change can be traced back to the writings and teachings of Simon Nelson Patten at the Wharton School:

    Rejecting the economics of scarcity, he (i.e. Patten) emphasized the abundance of nature and man's ability to exploit it. in his view, economics was not a dismal science "foretelling disaster and showing the fundamental limitations that are set on progress." It was, rather, a science of optimism that pointed the way to unending progress by showing man how to multiply nature through his intelligence. (1988, 25)

4. Interestingly, neither Columbia professor Rexford G. Tugwell, nor his works, especially *The Industrial Discipline and the Governmental Arts* (1933) are cited in Harold Moulton's work. Thus, there can be little doubt that he was familiar with the controversial Columbia University professor's views on the Great-Depression and the role of government in economic affairs.

5. The *Congressional Record* for the period March 1933 to June 1933 is replete with references to Professor Tugwell's *The Industrial Discipline and the Governmental Arts* (1933). Opponents, mostly Old-Guard Republicans, denounced his work as more radical (i.e. further to the left) than Karl Marx's *Das Capital.*

6. In his 1971 biography of Senator Robert F. Wagner, Joseph Huthmacher refers repeatedly to his close relationship with Professor Tugwell.

7. *Congressional Record,* June 7, 1933.

8. *The New York Times,* May 18, 1933.

9. *The New York Times,* August 17, 1933.

10. The New York Times, June 14, 1933.

11. In its ruling on Schechter Poultry Corporation versus the People of the United States, 295 U.S. 495-555, the Supreme Court held that:

    Extraordinary conditions do not create or enlarge constitution al power, and cannot justify governmental action outside the sphere of constitution al authority, that the powers of the National Government are limited to those granted by the Constitution, that legislative power is unconstitutionally delegated by the provisions of Section 3 of—the National Industrial Recovery Act of June 16, 1933 authorizing the making of codes for the government of trades and industries by or with the approval of the President of the United States without setting up standards aside from the statement of the general aim of rehabilitation, correction and development of trade and industries.

12. In June 1933, a reporter asked Ford: "Do you think the Industrial Recovery Bill, with the powers it vests in the President a useful economic measure?". He replied: "I see nothing in the program that has not been in our own program for years, with the exception of a few minor points" *(The New York Times,* June 16, 1933).

13. *The New York Times,* June 16, 1933.

14. The record shows, however, that Robert F. Wagner, like President Herbert C. Hoover, favored voluntary action. According to a story in *The New York Times Saturday Magazine* of June 11, 1933: The main differences were between General Hugh Johnson, who had been appointed to organize the work to be done under the bill, and Senator Wagner. Johnson wanted the army doctrine of force applied to the bill; Wagner placed the emphasis on cooperation. At this juncture, the President was

called upon to arbitrate. He told Wagner and Johnson and, of all people, Donald Richberg, counsel for the railroad unions, to get together in a room and agree. They did so and the bill as presented to Congress was the result. *(The New York Times,* June 11, 1933, Sunday Magazine)

15. John K. Galbraith, in *The Great Crash*, 1929 (1955) pointed to "the bad distribution of income that left the rich with too much for new investment and the poor with too little to buy" as one of the causes of the Great Depression.

16. Indirect evidence that the owners of capital had not captured all or even part of the technology shock-induced productivity gains comes in the form of Adolf Berle and Gardiner Means' *The Modern Corporation and Private Property* published in 1932 which decries shareholders' loss of control at the expense of managers. One could argue that had capital captured the lion's share of the productivity gain as Tugwell, Wagner and others contended, Berle and Means' critique of the "modern corporation" would have never been written. The late 1920s, it therefore follows, ought to be viewed as a period in which everyone (i.e. the owners of capital and labor) was aware of the fact that potential output had increased dramatically; however, neither understood why their real income had not increased. Labor blamed capital, and capital blamed managers.

CHAPTER 7

1. For an example, see Balke and Gordon (1986).

2. Klein and Preston (1967) alluded to a similar problem: "Some peaks may be marked off as full-capacity utilization peaks when in fact there may have been considerable underutilization of capacity" (1967, 54).

3. Another issue is the very nature of the technological change (i.e. labor-saving, capital-saving, or Hicks-neutral). Theoretically speaking, labor-saving technological change can be ruled out on the grounds that the real wage rate remained relatively constant from 1925 to 1929. Hicks-neutral technological change can be ruled out on similar grounds, leaving capital-saving technological change as the only alternative. Capital-saving technological change increases the labor-capital ratio, thus decreasing the wage-rental ratio. Since dividends track variations in the rental rate on

capital, it follows that the dividend growth in the 1924-1927 period referred to by White (1990) and others can only logically be attributed to capital-saving technological change. This, however, stands in stark contrast with the stylized facts. Specifically, most studies (see Jorgenson, Gollop and Fraumeni 1987 for a survey) have found technological change in this century to be of the labor-saving variety (see also Burmeister and Dobell 1969). That is, technological change has, for the most part, increased the capital-labor ratio.

4.   The long-run rate of growth of the labor force, n, was estimated using U.S. Department of Commerce data on non-agricultural employment for the period 1910-1960 (U.S. Department of Commerce 1975, series D127). The estimated equation is: $EMPL = 20,836.468e^{0.0185701t}$; $R^2 = .86940$; F(1,49)=333.8532. The estimate of n was found to be sensitive to the period chosen. By shortening the period, the value of n decreased. For example, for the period 1910-1950, the estimated value for n is .0159.

5.   Here, technological change is assumed to be of the Hicks-neutral variety.

6.   This is commonly referred to as the economic fundamentals hypothesis which holds that the intrinsic value of a share is based on both actual and potential earning power. For more on economic fundamentals, see Graham, Dodd, and Cottle (1962).

APPENDIX A

1. *The New York Times*, October 21, 1929.

2. *The New York Times*, October 21, 1929.

3. *The New York Times*, October 22, 1929.

4. *The New York Times*, October 22, 1929.

5. *The New York Times*, October 23, 1929.

6. *The New York Times*, October 25, 1929.

7. *The New York Times*, October 28, 1929.

8. *The New York Times,* October 29, 1929.

9. *The New York Times,* October 30, 1929

Bibliography

Abreu, Dilip, David Pearce, and Ennio Stachetti. 1986. Optimal Cartel Equilibria with Imperfect Monitoring. *Journal of Economic Theory* 39: 251-269.

Aldcroft, Derek H. 1970. *The Inter-War Economy:* Britain 1919-1939. London: B. T. Batsford.

Archibald, Chris, and Richard Lipsey. 1958. Monetary and Value Theory: A critique of Lange and Patinkin. *Review of Economic Studies.*

Balke, N.S. and Robert J. Gordon. 1986. Historical Data. in Robert J. Gordon, ed., *The American Business Cycle,* Chicago, IL: University of Chicago Press.

Barro, Robert J. 1972. A Theory of Monopolistic Price Adjustment. *Review of Economic Studies* 34: 17-26.

Barro, Robert J. and Herschel Grossman. 1976. *Money, Employment and Inflation.* Cambridge: Cambridge University Press.

Barsky, Richard B., and J. Bradford De Long. 1990. Bull and Bear Markets in the Twentieth Century. *Journal of Economic History* 50: 265-282.

Beaudreau, Bernard C. 1983. Technology-Induced Growth, Sequential Monetary Exchange and the Free-Rider Problem. Mimeo, University of Western Ontario.

Beaudreau, Bernard C. 1995a. The Impact of Electric Power on Productivity: A Study of U .S. Manufacturing 1950-1984. *Energy Economics* 17: 231-236.

Beaudreau, Bernard C.1995b. Newtonian Production Processes. Mimeo, Université Laval.

Beaudreau, Bernard C. 1996a. *Mass Production, The Stock Market Crash, and The Great Depression: The Macroeconomics of Electrification.* Westport, CT: Greenwood Press.

Beaudreau, Bernard C. 1996b. R&D: To Compete or to Cooperate. *Economics of Innovation and New Technology* 4:173–186.

Beaudreau, Bernard C. 1998. *Energy and Organization: Growth and Distribution Reexamined.* Westport, CT: Greenwood Press.

Beaudreau, Bernard C. 1999. *Energy and the Rise and Fall of Political Economy.* Westport, CT: Greenwood Press.

Beaudreau, Bernard C. 1999b. Electric Power, Keynes, and the $4.86 Pound: A Reexamination of Britain's Return to the Gold Standard. *Journal of European Economic History.* 28: 383-408.

Beaudreau, Bernard C. 2004. *Making Markets and Making Money: Strategy and Monetary Exchange.* New York, NY: iUniverse.

Beaudreau, Bernard C. 2005. On the Emergence and Evolution of Economic Complexity, Department of Economics, Université Laval.

Bell, Spurgeon. 1940. *Productivity, Wages and National Income.* Washington, DC: Brookings Institution...

Benassy, Jean Pierre. 1975. Neo-Keynesian Disequilibrium Theory in a Monetary Economy. *Review of Economic Studies* 42: 503-523.

Berle, Adolf A., and Gardiner C. Means. 1932. *The Modern Corporation and Private Property.* New York, NY: MacMillan.

Bernanke, Ben S. 1986."Employment, Hours and Earnings in the Depression." *American Economic Review* 76: 82-109.

Bernanke, Ben S. 1994. The Macroeconomics of the Great Depression: A Comparative Approach. Working Paper No. 4814, *National Bureau of Economic Research.*

Bernstein, Michael A. 1987. *The Great Depression: Delayed Recovery and Economic Change in America* 1929-1939. Cambridge: Cambridge University Press.

Blanchard, Olivier J., and Nobuhiro Kiyotaki. 1987. Monopolistic Competition and the Effects of Aggregate Demand." *American Economic Review* 77: 647-666.

Blanchard, Olivier J. and Stanley Fischer. 1990. *Lectures on Macroeconomics.* Cambridge, MA: Massachusetts Institute of Technology Press...

Brown, William A. 1940. *The International Gold Standard Reinterpreted.* New York: AMS Press.

Burmeister Edwin, and Richard Dobell. 1969. Disembodied Technological Change with Many Factors. *Journal of Economic Theory* 1: 1-8.

Campbell, John, and N. Gregory Mankiw. 1987. Permanent and Transitory Components in Macroeconomic Fluctuations. *American Economic Review* 77: 111-117.

Carver, Thomas Nixon. 1925. *The Present Economic Revolution in the United States.* Boston: Little, Brown and Company.

Clapham, Sir John. *An Economic History of Modern Britain.* Cambridge: Cambridge University Press, 1951.

Clower Robert W. *Economic Doctrine and Method: Selected Papers of R. W. Clower.* Aldershot. Edward Elgar Publishing Co. 1995.

Clower, Robert and Peter Howitt. 2000. The Emergence of Economic Organization. *Journal of Economic Behavior and Organization* 41: 55-84.

Cooper, Russell, and Andrew John.1988. Coordinating Coordination Failures in Keynesian Models. *Quarterly Journal of Economics* 103: 441-464.

Dearing, Charles L., Paul T. Homan, Lewis L. Lorwin, and Leverett S. Lyon. 1934. *The ABC of the NRA.* Washington, DC: Brookings Institution.

Destler, I.M. 1986. *American Trade Policies : System Under Stress.* Washington, DC : Institute for International Economics. *American Trade Policies:*

Devine, Warren D., Jr. 1990. Electrified Mechanical Drive: The Historical Power Distribution Revolution. in Sam H. Schurr, Calin C. Burwell, Warren D. Devine, Jr., and Sidney Sonenblum, eds. *Electricity in the American Economy: Agent of Technological Progress.* Westport, CT: Greenwood Press.

Diamond, Peter. 1982. Aggregate Demand Management in Search Equilibrium. *Journal of Political Economy* 90: 881-894.

Diamond, Peter. 1984. *A Search Equilibrium Approach to the Microfoundations of Macroeconomics.* Cambridge, MA: MIT Press.

Douglas, Clifford H. 1933. *Social Credit.* New York, NY: W.W. Norton and Company.

Douglas, Clifford H. 1951. *The Monopoly of Credit.* Liverpool: K.R.P. Publications.

Du Boff, Richard B. 1967. The Introduction of Electric Power in American Manufacturing. *Economic History Review*: 509-518.

Ewen, Stuart. 1976. *Captains of Conciousness.* New York: McGraw-Hill.

Farmer, Roger E.A. 1996. *Macroeconomics of Self-Fulfilling Prophecies.* Cambridge, MA: MIT Press.

Faulkner, Harold U. 1950. *From Versailles to the New Deal.* New Haven, CT: Yale University Press.

Filene, Edward A. 1923. The Minimum Wage and Efficiency. *American Economic Review* 13: 411-415.

Filene, Edward A. 1924. *The Way Out: A Forecast of Coming Changes in American Business and Industry.* New York: Doubleday, Page and Co.

Filene, Edward A. 1929. Mass Production Makes a Better World. *Atlantic Monthly* 143: 625-631.

Filene, Edward A. 1931. *Successful Living in This Machine Age.* New York: Simon and Schuster.

Filipetti, George, and Roland Vaile. 1935. *The Economic Effects of the NRA: A Regional Analysis.* Minneapolis: University of Minnesota Press.

Fine, Sidney. 1963. *The Automobile under the Blue Eagle.* Ann Arbor, MÌ: University of Michigan Press.

Finley, Moses I. 1973. *The Ancient Economy.* Berkeley, CA: University of California Press.

Fisher, Irving. 1930. *The Stock Market Crash and After.* New York, NY: Macmillan.

Flora, Peter, Franz Kraus, and Winifried Pfenning. 1987. *State, Economy and Society in Western Europe* 1815-1975. Frankfurt, Germany: Campus Verlag.

Foot, M.D.K.W.1972. The Balance of Payments in the Interwar Years. *The Bank of England Quarterly Review* 12: 345-363.

Ford, Henry. 1922. *My Life and Work.* Garden City, NY: Garden City Publishing Co.

Ford, Henry. 1926a. *Today and Tomorrow.* New York, NY: Doubleday.

Ford, Henry. 1926b. Mass Production. *Encyclopaedia Britannica* 13: 821-823.

Friedman, Milton, and Anna J. Schwartz. 1963. *A Monetary History of the United States 1867-1960.* New York: National Bureau of Economic Research.

Fudenberg, Drew, and Jean Tirole. 1992. *Game Theory.* Cambridge, MA: MIT Press.

Galbraith, John K. 1955. *The Great Crash,* 1929. Boston, MA: Houghton Mifflin Company.

Gordon, Robert J. 1990. What is New-Keynesian Economics? *Journal of Economic Literature* 28: 1115-1171.

Graham, Benjamin, David L. Dodd, and Sidney Cottle. 1962. *Security Analysis: Principles and Techniques.* New York, NY: McGraw-Hill.

Green, Edward J., and Robert H. Porter. 1984. Non-Cooperative Collusion Under Imperfect Price Information. *Econometrica* 52: 87-100.

Hardach, Karl. 1980. *The Political Economy of Germany in the 20th Century.* Berkeley, CA: University of California Press.

Hawley, Ellis W. 1976. Antitrust on the Defensive: The American Movement for a Cartelized Economy. *Review of American History* 4: 582-587.

Hawley. Ellis W. 1979. *The Great War and the Search for a Modern Order: A History of the American People and Their Institutions. 1917-1933.* New York, NY: St. Martin's Press.

Heaton, Herbert. 1948.*The Economic History of Europe.* New York, NY: Harper and Row.

Heller, Walter P. 1986. Coordination Failure under Complete Markets with Applications to Effective Demand. in Walter P. Heller *et al.* eds. *Equilibrium Analysis: Essays in Honor of Kenneth J. Arrow.* Cambridge: Cambridge University Press.

Henderson, James M. and Richard E. Quandt. 1980. *Microeconomic Theory.* New York, NY: McGraw Hill.

Hicks, John. 1935. A Suggestion for Simplifying the Theory of Money. *Economica.*

Hicks, John D. 1960. *Normalcy and Reaction* 1921-1933. Washington, DC: Service Center for Teachers of History.

Garnsey, P. K. Hopkins and C.R. Whittaker. 1983. *Trade in the Ancient Economy,* London.

Hounshell, David A. 1984. *From the American System to Mass Production 1800-1932.* Baltimore, Md.: The Johns Hopkins University Press.

Huthmacher, J. Joseph. 1971. *Senator Robert F. Wagner and the Rise of Urban Liberalism.* New York, NY: Atheneum.

Inglis, Brian. 1971. *Men of Conscience.* New York, NY: Macmillan.

Johnson, Hugh J. 1935. *The Blue Eagle: From Egg to Earth.* New Garden City, NY: Doubleday, Doran and Company...

Jorgenson, Dale W., Frank M. Gollop, and Barbara M. Fraumeni. 1987. *Productivity and U.S. Economic Growth.* Cambridge, MA: Harvard University Press.

Keller, Robert E. 1973. Factor Income Distribution in the United States during the 1920s: A Reexamination of Fact and Theory. *Journal of Economic History*: 252-273.

Keynes, John M. 1936. *The General Theory of Employment, Interest and Money.* London: Macmillan.

Kindersley, Charles. 1931. British Foreign Investment in 1929. *Economic Journal*: 370-384.

Kindleberger, Charles P. 1973. *The World Depression* 1929-1939. Berkeley, CA: University of California Press.

King, Williford I. 1920. Circulating Capital: Its Nature and Relation to Public Welfare. *American Economic Review* 10(4): 738-754.

King, Robert G., and Charles I. Plosser. 1984. Money, Credit and Prices in a Real Business Cycle. *American Economic Review* 74: 363-380.

Klein, Laurence R., and R. Preston. 1967. New Results in the Measurement of Capacity Utilization. *American Economic Review* 57: 34-58.

Knight, K. G. 1987. *Unemployment: An Economic Analysis.* London: Croom Helm.

Kuenne, Robert E. 1986. Rivalrous Consonance: *A Theory of General Oligopolistic Equilibrium* New York: North-Holland.

Lacey, Robert. 1986. *Ford: The Men and the Machine.* Boston, MA: Little Brown and Company.

Laidler, David. 1977. *The Demand for Money: Theories and Evidence*. New York, NY: Dun-Donnelley.

Laidler, David. 1990. *Taking Money Seriously and Other Essays*. Cambridge, MA: MIT Press.

Laidler, David. 1993. *The Demand for Money: Theories, Evidence and Problems* . New York, NY: HarperCollins College Publishers.

Leijonhufvud, Axel. 1981. *Information and Coordination: Essays in Macroeconomic Theory*. New York, NY: Oxford University Press.

Levin, Maurice, Harold G. Moulton, and Clark Warburton. 1934. *America's Capacity to Consume*. Washington, DC: Brookings Institution.

Lippman, Steven A., and John J. McCall. 1976. The Economics of Job Search." *Economic Inquiry* 14: 155-189.

Long, John B., and Charles I. Plosser. 1983. Real Business Cycles. *Journal of Political Economy* 91: 39-69.

Lyon, Leverett S., Paul T. Homan, Lewis L. Lorwin, George Terborg, Charles L Dearing, and Leon C. Marshall. 1935. *The National Recovery Administration: An Analysis and Appraisal*. Washington, DC: Brookings Institution.

MacKinnon, Keith T. 1987. More on the Inflation Tax and the Value of Equity. *Canadian Journal of Economics* 20: 823-831.

Malthus, Thomas. 1827. *Principles of Political Economy*. New York, NY: Augustus M. Kelley.

Mason, Edward S. 1934. Controlling Industry. in D. V. Brown, ed., *The Economics of the Recovery Program*. New York, NY: DaCapo Press.

Means, Gardiner C. 1939. *The Structure of the U.S. Economy*. Washington, DC: U.S. Government Printing Office for the National Resource Committee.

Meek, Ronald L. 1951. Physiocracy and the Early Theories of Under-Consumption. *Economica* 18: 229-269.

Meltzer, Alan 1976. Monetary and Other Explanations of the Start of the Great Depression. *Journal of Monetary Economics* 2: 455-471.

Merill, Milton R. 1990. *Reed Smoot: Apostle in Politics*. Logan, UT: Utah State Press.

Mitchell, Broadus. 1992. *Depression Decade*. New York: Holt, Rinehart and Winston, 1947. Mitchell, B. R. *International Historical Statistics Europe, 1750-1988*. London: Stockton Press.

Moulton, Harold G. 1935. *Income and Economic Progress*. Washington DC: The Brookings Institution.

Moulton, Harold G. 1938 *Financial Organization and the Economic System*. New York, NY: McGraw-Hill.

Mummery, A. F. and John A. Hobson. 1889. *The Physiology of Industry*. London: John Murray.

Namorato, Michael. 1988. *Rexford G. Tugwell*. New York, NY: Praeger Press.

National Bureau of Economic Research. 1929. *Recent Economic Changes in the United States*. New York, NY: McGraw Hill.

National Industrial Conference Board. 1943. *The Economic Almanac for* 1943-1944. New York, NY: National Industrial Conference Board.

Nearing, Scott. 1952. *Economics for the Power Age*. New York, NY: John Day Co.

Nelson, Charles and Charles Plosser. 1982. Trends and Random Walks in Macroeconomic Time Series. *Journal of Monetary Economics* 10: 139-162.

Nevins, Allan. 1954. *Ford: The Times, The Man, The Company*. New York, NY: Charles Scribner's Sons.

Nevins, Allan, and Frank Ernest Hill. 1957. *Ford: Expansion and Challenge, 1915-1933*. New York, NY: Charles Scribner's Sons.

Nourse, Edwin A., and Associates. 1934. *America's Capacity to Produce.* Washington DC: Brookings Institution.

Okun, Arthur. 1962. Potential GNP: Its Measurement and Significance. in 1962 *Proceedings of the Business and Statistics Section.*

Osborne, David K. 1976. Cartel Problems. *American Economic Review* 66: 835-844.

Owen, Robert. 1858. *The Life of Robert Owen.* New York, NY: Augustus Kelley.

Pasdermadjian, H. 1959. *La deuxieme revolution industrielle.* Paris: Presses Universitaires de France.

Pastor, Robert. 1980. *Congress and the Politics of United States Foreign Economic Policy, 1929-1976.* Berkeley, CA: University of California Press.

Patinkin, Don. 1965. *Money, Interest and Prices.* New York, NY: Harper and Row.

Pierce, Phyllis S. 1991. *The Dow Jones Averages 1885-1990.* Homewood, IL: Business One Irwin.

Pigou, Arthur C. 1917. The Value of Money. *Quarterly Journal of Economics,* 37(4): 38–65.

Pigou, Arthur C. 1949. *The Veil of Money.* London: Macmillan and Co.

Pollard, Sidney. 1962. *The Development of the British Economy 1914-1950.* London: Edward Arnold.

Porter, Robert H. 1983. Optimal Cartel Trigger Price Strategies. *Journal of Economic Theory* 29: 313-338.

Prescott, Edward. 1986. Theory Ahead of Business Cycle Measurement. *Federal Reserve Bank of Minneapolis Quarterly Review* 10: 9-22.

Raff, Daniel M. G., and Lawrence Summers. 1987. Did Henry Ford Pay Efficiency Wages? *Journal of Labor Economics* 5: S57-S86.

Ricardo, David, 1817. The Principles of Political Economy and Taxation (New York, NY: Everyman's Library (1965).

Roberts, John. 1987. An Equilibrium Model of Involuntary Unemployment at Flexible, Competitive Prices and Wages. *American Economic Review* 77: 856-874.

Robertson, Ross M. 1973. *History of the American Economy*. New York, NY: Harcourt, Brace and Jovanovich.

Robinson, E. E. 1958. *The Roosevelt Leadership 1933-1945*. New York, NY: J. B. Lippincott Co.

Rogin, Leo. 1935. The New Deal: Survey of the Literature. *Quarterly Journal of Economics* 49: 325-355.

Romasco, Albert U. 1983. *The Politics of Recovery*. New York, NY: Oxford University Press.

Roose, Kenneth. 1954. *The Economic Recession and Revival*. New Haven, CT: Yale University Press.

Rosenberg, Nathan. 1972. *Technology and American Economic Growth*. Armonk, NY: M. E. Sharpe.

Rosenberg, Nathan, and L. E. Birdzell, Jr. 1986. *How the West Grew Rich: The Transformation of the Industrial World*. New York, NY: Basic Books.

Schumpeter, Joseph A. 1946. The American Economy in the Interwar Period: The Decade of the Twenties. *American Economic Review Papers and Proceedings*: 1-10.

Schurr, Sam H., Calvin C. Burwell, Warren D. Devine, Jr., and Sidney Sonenblum, eds. 1990. *Electricity in the American Economy: Agent of Technological Progress*. Westport, CT: Greenwood Press.

Scott, Howard et al. 1933. *Introduction to Technocracy*. New York, NY: The John Day Company.

Self, Sir Henry, and Elizabeth M. Watson. 1952. *Electricity Supply in Great Britain*. London: George Allen and Unwin.

Shapiro, Matthew O. 1987. Are Cyclical Fluctuations in Productivity Due More to Supply Shocks or Demand Shocks? *American Economic Review* 77: 118-124.

Shattschneider, E.E. 1935. *Politics, Pressures, and the Tariff.* New York, NY: Prentice Hall.

Shiller, Robert J. 1981. "Do Stock Prices Move Too Much to Be Justified by Subsequent Changes in Dividends?" *American Economic Review* 71: 421-436.

Sirkin, Gerald. 1975. The Stock Market of 1929 Revisited: A Note. *Business History Review*: 233-241.

Sismonde de Sismondi, Jean-Charles Léonard. 1819. *Nouveaux principes d'économie politique.* Paris: Calmann-Levy.

Sonenblum, Sidney. 1990. Electrification and Productivity Growth in Manufacturing. in Sam H. Schurr, Calvin C. Burwell, Warren D. Devine, Jr., and Sidney Sonenblum, eds. *Electricity in the American Economy: Agent of Technological Progess.* Westport, CT: Greenwood Press.

Sowell, Thomas. 1972. *Say's Law: An Historical Analysis.* Princeton, NJ: Princeton University Press.

Stiglitz, Joseph E. 1990. Symposium on Bubbles. *Journal of Economic Perspectives* 4: 13-18.

Taussig, Frank. 1930. The Tariff, 1929-1930. *The Quarterly Journal of Economics* 44: 175-204.

Temin, Peter. 1976. *Did Monetary Forces Cause the Great Depression?* New York, NY: Norton.

Temin, Peter. 1990. Socialism and Wages in the Recovery from the Great Depression in the United States and Germany. *Journal of Economic History* 50: 297-308.

Temin, Peter. 1991. *Lessons from the Great Depression.* Cambridge, MA: Massachusetts Institute of Technology Press.

Tugwell, Rexford G. 1927. *Industry's Coming of Age*. New York, NY: Columbia University Press.

Tugwell, Rexford G. 1933. *The Industrial Discipline and the Governmental Arts*. New York, NY: Columbia University Press.

U.S. Department of Commerce. 1932. *Survey of Current Business-Annual Supplement* 1932. Washington, DC: U.S. Government Printing Office.

U.S. Department of Commerce. 1975. *Historical Statistics of the U.S.: Colonial Times to 1970*. Washington, DC: U.S. Government Printing Office.

Uzawa, H. 1961. On a Two-Sector Model of Economic Growth and Technical Progress. *Review of Economic Studies* 23: 40-50.

Varian, Hal R. 1992. *Microeconomic Analysis*. New York, NY: Norton.

Ware, R. G. 1974. The Inter-War Years. *The Bank of England Quarterly Review:* 47-52.

Weinstein, Michael. 1980. *Recovery and Redistribution under the NIRA*. New York: North Holland.

White, Eugene N. 1990. The Stock Market Boom and Crash of 1929 Revisited. *Journal of Economic Perspectives* 4. 67-83.

White, William J. 2000. "An Unsung Hero: The Farm Tractor's Contribution to Twentieth-century United States Economic Growth." Ph.D. dissertation, Ohio State University.

Wicksell, Knut. 1898. *Interest and Prices: A Study of the Causes Regulating the Value of Money*. London: Macmillan and Co.

978-0-595-37888-3
0-595-37888-9